Tigran Gyozalyan

The King
Is a Powerful Piece

MONGOOSE
Press

BOSTON

Publisher: Mongoose Press
1005 Boylston Street, Suite 324
Newton Highlands, MA 02461
info@mongoosepress.com
www.MongoosePress.com

ISBN: 978-1-936277-80-3
Library of Congress Control Number: 2017907832

Distributed to the trade by National Book Network
custserv@nbnbooks.com, 800-462-6420
For all other sales inquiries please contact the Publisher.

Layout: Stanislav Makarov
Editor: Jorge Amador
Cover Design: Alexander Krivenda
Printed in the United States of America

First English edition
0 9 8 7 6 5 4 3 2 1

Contents

Foreword

I have known Tigran Gyozalyan almost since I started playing chess. Living in Vanadzor, Armenia, Tigran was highly respected in Yerevan's Central Chess Club, and whenever he would attend the Armenian Championship in the capital, with all of his students, he would always be most warmly received. And, considering that he is quite a well-read and sensitive soul, he has always been sought after as a conversationalist who would freely offer advice to my family and me in my growing years. Most of Tigran's students share certain important qualities: they are well educated and fearless. One of my seconds – as well as my friend – the grandmaster Samvel Ter-Sahakyan, possesses these good qualities, both as a player and a person, because he is Gyozalyan's student.

The theory the author presents was first introduced into practice by the very first world chess champion, Wilhelm Steinitz. Back then it was absolutely a brand-new idea, especially in a time when players would sacrifice a whole board's worth of pieces to drive the enemy king out for a walk. So Steinitz's idea was taken with a large grain of salt. Indeed, who ever heard of the king's taking care of itself?! It was a long time before players began to make use of the unguarded king; but even today, you can still see grandmasters who are afraid to leave their king in the center. This book shines a bright light on this rare theme; I hope that the reader will find inside it much that is new and unexpected about our beloved game.

Levon Aronian, GM
Yerevan (Armenia), August 2016

Preface

As a professional who has spent his whole life in the service of chess, and who continues serving chess as a trainer, I face a very important question – how do we combat and break down chess stereotypes? One of the chief stereotypes that a trainer must break in his young students in the early stages of training, is that the king is merely the weakest piece and requires constant protection. In later stages of training, this stereotype gets diluted somewhat as the trainer begins to explain endgame theory, as the king plays the decisive role in most cases. But here this is easy to understand: there aren't a lot of pieces around, you can see that.

Starting in childhood, we are told that "A" is good while "B" is bad. That motto stays with us throughout our lives, whereas deep inside we often know that in this concrete situation "B" doesn't look so bad, but "A" might lead to disaster. So it's hard to make up our minds, because we haven't learned to get rid of the stereotype. In this work, Tigran Gyozalyan presents many remarkable examples to combat the stereotype of the "weak king." The most successful people on this planet are those who have overcome conventional thinking; and there are many examples – even people like the late Steve Jobs, who showed by his very existence the success of the algorithm of unfettered thought.

In this beautiful book, there are numerous examples of how the king behaves depending on the circumstances. When there are weaknesses in his camp, then he has to be the defender who takes care of his own world; when he lacks the resources to carry out the attack, he marches forward like a good soldier, instead of cowering in the rear, the way all the rules for playing good chess advise us to do; when the enemy's artillery is smashing his fortress open, then he should find safe shelter, that he might save the honor of his army. I well understand what a laborious task it was for Tigran to gather and sort through the mass of available material. This enormously difficult job may truly be compared to prospecting for oil: so many "dry holes" before you hit on the "black gold," and you can taste the drillers' joy! This may be compared to the joy experienced by my friend Tigran Gyozalyan, the first to explore this complex theme of the king's role in the early and middle stages of the game.

I extend my heartfelt congratulations to Tigran for this outstanding book, and I recommend it to every methodical trainer working with chessplayers from 1600 level to candidate master. Let them use it to break down childhood stereotypes. But I also recommend it to all chessplayers, to broaden our horizons and enrich our thinking!

Zurab Azmaiparashvili, GM
President, European Chess Union

Introduction

The role of the king in the endgame is well known. Much is known and much has been said about it – especially well so by Mikhail Shereshevsky in his classic manual, *Endgame Strategy*.

But what role does the king play in complex middlegame positions, or even in the opening? Let's be honest: whenever we see the king in such situations, we cannot remain neutral about it, and with good reason. For the king is the most contradictory of all the pieces. On the one hand, we need to protect and preserve it; and yet, on the other hand it's quite logical to exploit its strengths – after all, it's still a piece.

In this book, for the first time, the reader is presented with a systematic treatment of what the king can accomplish in complex middlegame and opening situations.

How did we come up with the idea to write about this? First, because up until now, chess theory has lacked a classification of the various ways to use the king in complex positions. And without such a classification, you can't call it a teachable theme.

So, as a trainer myself, I was interested in determining whether I could I fill this gap in the chess literature. Classifiable material is subject to methodological rules: it's easily passed on from trainer to students, and it is absorbed well by the latter. The learning process is a productive one.

In addition, this intriguing theme is not well studied. In practice, we rarely encounter situations where the king may become active in complex opening and/or middlegame positions. Out of tens of thousands of games examined, I've managed to collect only a handful of examples, which bears witness to the uniqueness of this theme. As this theme has been addressed only rarely in the chess literature, we want to fill the gap.

The first volume of Mark Dvoretsky's "School of Future Champions" series, *Secrets of Chess Training*, includes a lecture ("A Feeling for the King" by Gregory Kaidanov, with additional material by Artur Yusupov and by Dvoretsky himself) which touches on this. The examples presented by the authors were quite interesting. However, not being laid out systematically, they proved rather scattershot – sometimes, endgame examples were chosen, which is a horse of a different color entirely!

The Russian trainer Anatoly Terekhin, in one section of his fine book, *Strategic Techniques in Chess*, dealt only with the theme of escaping with the king. He split this properly into two parts: 1) ahead of its own pawn phalanx; and 2) away from enemy attack.

But I knew about the theme of royal escapes in this format long before Terekhin's book. I even had a notebook, containing notes from a lecture by Boris Zlotnik – who was at that time a Senior Professor in the Chess Department at the Russian State University of Physical Education, Sport, Youth, and Tourism (GTsOLIFK) – on this theme of the king escaping. Boris Anatolievich showed a pair of games by Tigran Petrosian, one against GM Jesús Díez del Corral, and the other against GM Wolfgang Unzicker. In the former, Petrosian escaped with his king from White's attack; in the latter, his king ran away ahead of his own pawn storm. These two games are given in the chapters on evacuating one's king.

The other reason why I chose this theme is that it's so unusual, and so especially fascinating for chessplayers. On the chessboard, it seldom happens that we are forced to act in an original fashion, without preconceptions. And the king may become a full participant in the struggle, unexpectedly lending its own powerful presence to the contest. You will agree that this cannot help but be attractive to anyone who truly values chess as an art form.

We know that the first known personality in chess history to give serious attention to the particulars of king play in complex middlegame positions was the brilliant Wilhelm Steinitz, the first player to bear the title of World Champion. It will suffice to recall his highly original invention in the Vienna Game, where as early as on move 5 his king gives up castling voluntarily! (The reader will learn more about this in Chapter 8.)

Let me suggest a reason why Steinitz would consider aspects of king play that had hitherto not been sufficiently considered. I will lay out my thoughts in a few words.

In the Romantic Period of Adolf Anderssen and the early Steinitz, the king was the object of direct attack in nearly every game; and in most cases, they got to him. Steinitz's sharp eye singled out those moments when it wasn't enough for the king to settle for the role of passive observer and might very well take an active part in the struggle, to the benefit of its own army. As a result, he presented a new formula to the chess world: "The king is a strong piece!" That is, just like the rest of the pieces. Steinitz encouraged others, not merely to limit themselves to thinking about how to protect the king, but also about how to exploit its power, at the right moment.

This was a truly revolutionary idea! Steinitz made the chess world reconsider how to handle the king in complex positions. We need only find a situation where it could perform active duty: use its strengths just as we would any other piece. We should only observe proper restraint – much as with any other piece. Once again: this can only be done under exceptional circumstances.

I feel confident – and this is supported by my experience as a trainer – that a chessplayer can develop a feel for handling the king along with other playing qualities. I also hope that this work will be appreciated by all who value the art of chess. (Here, we will not discuss such commonly seen types of king play as prophylaxis, quiet moves, and the like.)

Any published work requires completeness. So your author will gladly welcome corrections for the bulk of the work, as well as interesting suggestions or additions to the theme. In addition, I would like to note that the exercises in the final section are not presented as some sort of test, but rather as a study theme. I also hope that this work will prove a valuable teaching aid for trainers, and that the illustrative games – and this is most important – will give true joy to all who value the art of chess.

The author is grateful for the help with this book provided by International Masters Ashot Nadanian and Tibor Károlyi.

Tigran Gyozalyan
Singapore, October 2016

Chapter 1

The Aggressive King

It doesn't happen very often, but it *does* happen once in a while that one player's king can play a part in checkmating its counterpart.

As a rule, this only happens:

a) when the opposing forces are so restricted that they have no active counterplay;

b) when the king, extricating itself from its pursuers' attack, approaches its rival so closely that he can the dot the "i"; or

c) in a double-edged position, when the king itself takes the initiative and, instead of seeking shelter, gradually draws closer to its opponent.

In the latter two cases, the king often combines defense and attack.

Without a doubt, the study by the brilliant Sam Loyd, dedicated to Steinitz – which you will find at the end of this book in the problems section – provides a beautiful illustration of our theme.

Note also that the king's unexpected aggressiveness will have shock value against the opponent. A sharp change in circumstances can knock any player for a loop, greatly increasing the chances of his making a mistake.

The game below is far from the earliest known example of our theme. A position like this one occurred in a Steinitz–Zukertort game from London 1872; we will examine that game in our chapter on deliberately giving up the right to castle.

1. R. Teichmann – Allies

Glasgow 1902

I dare say that this is the best-known game of this sort. I remember first seeing it as a youngster. White's idea truly blew me away. To this day, I marvel at Rudolf Teichmann's imagination!

White has the better position, thanks to his beautifully placed knight: by controlling the important f7 and e8 squares, it cuts off Black's rook from the rest of its army, securing his queen's location at e7. The light squares in Black's camp are weak, too – especially the g6 square. He only needs to add his rook to the attack, and Black's position collapses. But how to do this? For Black has his own trumps – the queen-and-bishop battery, for one.

The white king takes an unexpected stroll, not only escaping this terrible battery, but also joining in the attack itself. As a side benefit, this frees up White's rook. Analysis shows that, with correct play, Black could have saved the game. However, as we have noted already, an aggressive king has a shocking effect on one's opponent; and so Black starts to go astray.

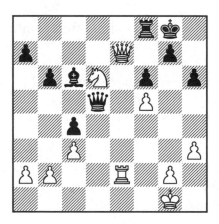

1.♔h2! b5

Here and on the next move, White could have played pragmatically with ♕e6+, with advantage; but to our great enjoyment, GM Teichmann at heart was more poet than scientist: he plans to march his king clear to g6!

2.♔g3!? a5

Black fails to sense the danger. By continuing with 2...♕d3+! 3.♔h4 (3.♔f2 a6) 3...♔h7!!, he might have improved the positions of both his king and rook and prevented White's attack: 4.♖e3 ♕d2 5.♖g3 ♖g8 when, apparently, this is one of those positions in which neither side can improve the position of his pieces, so dynamic equilibrium is maintained. But, you will agree, 3...♔h7 is not at all obvious.

3.♔h4!? g6

Black has been knocked for a loop. First he stops the king, then the rook; but he's helpless against the pawn. For those who love analysis, we offer the following variations for you to examine:

a) 3...♕c5 4.g4 ♕g1 5.♕c7 with a decisive penetration by the rook to the seventh rank;

b) 3...♖b8 4.♕c7 (not 4.♔h5?? ♖e8 – and suddenly it is *Black* who wins!) 4...♖f8 5.g4! ♔h7 6.♖e7 ♖g8 7.♘e4 wins;

c) 3...♖a8 (best) 4.♕e6+ ♕xe6 5.fxe6 ♖d8 6.♖d2!, with clearly better play.

4.♖e3 ♕xg2

On 4...♕c5, 5.g4 (with the idea of taking on g6) would be strong for White. Black would have no useful moves here; after something like 5...♗a8, White plays 6.fxg6 ♕g5+ 7.♔g3 ♕xg6 8.♘f5 h5 9.♕d6, and again there's no satisfactory defense to the threat of the white rook's invasion at e7.

We note also that a nice endgame awaits White after 5.♖g3 g5+ 6.♔h5 ♕e5 7.♖e3 ♕xe7 8.♖xe7 ♖d8 9.♘b7 ♖d7 10.♖xd7 ♗xd7 11.♔xh6 ♗xf5 12.♘d6, with an obvious advantage.

5.♖g3 ♕f2

If 5...g5+, then 6.♔h5 ♕xg3 7.♔g6:

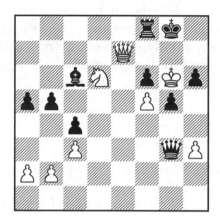

6.fxg6 ♕f4+ 7.♖g4 ♕f2+ 8.♔h5 1-0

Almost ninety (!) years later, the same "king fling" occurred in a game between two prominent contemporary grandmasters: the same queen + bishop combo, the same weak-square complex – only this time, the action took place on the dark squares.

It would be interesting to know whether Nigel Short knew about Teichmann's game. From my own experience as a trainer, I know that students will generally find the king's aggressive forward march fairly easily, once they remember the Teichmann game.

2. N. Short – J. Timman

Tilburg 1991

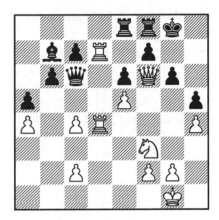

White's advantage is indisputable. There are probably a lot of strong continuations here. But the way that GM Short chose was, without a doubt, the strongest – and original as well.

31.♔h2!

The most spectacular.

31...♖c8

Black plays a waiting move, apparently mistaking White's last move as itself a waiting move. He only came to realize what was really going on when the white king was breathing down his neck.

Truth be told, it was already too late for Black to save himself; although, from a practical standpoint, unquestionably it would have been a good idea to take his last chance. I'm talking about 31...♗c8:

all the more so in that White would still need to show exceptional resourcefulness, which he could only do by playing 37.♖d2!! (see the comments at the end of the game).

Now, we have seen that the king's march into the enemy king's den, in this example and the previous one, was only rendered possible at all, as we chessplayers put it, by a sort of stalemating of the enemy pieces – in other words, when there is no strong counterplay. I sometimes refer to this condition as, "frozen pieces."

32.♔g3! ♖ce8 33.♔f4! ♗c8 34.♔g5! 1-0

If 34...♗xd7, then 35.♔h6 mates:

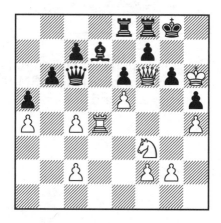

Now I'd like to present the following variations:

31...♗c8 32.g4! hxg4, otherwise:

a) 32...♗xd7 33.gxh5 wins;

b) 32...♗b7 33.♖d3 ♕e4 34.gxh5 ♕f5 35.♘g5 ♗c6 (35...♕g4 36.♖g3 ♕xh4+ 37.♖h3 ♕g4 38.f3) 36.♖xc7, and the win is not far off.

33.♘g5 ♗xd7 34.h5! g3+ 35.fxg3 ♕xa4 36.h6 ♕xc2+ 37.♖d2!!:

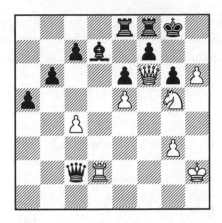

37...♛xd2+ 38.♔h3 – time for Black to resign, what do you think?

As for 37.♜d2!!, I assume that Timman was familiar with the outstanding study by A. Herbstmann and G. Nadareishvili (published in *Shakhmatnaya Moskva*, 1968, 1st prize), where White's bishop has just captured a black pawn on d4:

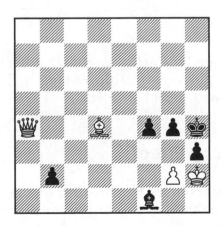

Black to move – White draws

1...g3+ 2.♔g1 h2+ 3.♔h1 ♝xg2+ 4.♔xg2 f3+ 5.♔h1 b1♛+ 6.♝g1+ ♛b4!!

Black sacrifices his own queen, simply to change the color of the white queen's diagonal! And now it is White, with his overwhelming preponderance of material, who must fight for the draw. A truly unique situation!

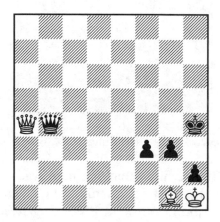

7.♕xb4+ ♔h3 8.♗xh2 f2 9.♕h4+!! ♔xh4 10.♗xg3+ ♔xg3

Stalemate!

A remarkable study! Finally, we note that the idea – interference, plus the simultaneous sacrifice of a major piece – belongs to the chess composer Leopold Mitrofanov.

The Boomerang Effect

In our first two examples, we noted that the aggressive king was possible only because the other side was somewhat restricted and had no active counterplay.

Now we move on to cases where the attacker lures the opposing king out of its fortress. In the heat of battle, if the attacker underestimates the defending king's hidden possibilities, then the latter can turn from prey into predator! Getting close to its opposite number, it'll become a threatening piece itself. Even during the most dangerous of attacks, one must always maintain a sense of proportion.

In games featuring this theme, we often see the king undertaking a lengthy voyage – a risky but also quite entertaining one! Both sides make mistakes, but the spectacle doesn't suffer in the least from that. What can you do – people are liable to make mistakes, and all the more so when the situation is fraught with tension!

See how a king, sword in hand, can sow terror in the opposing ranks!

3. Shtel – NN

Calcutta (now Kolkata) 1886

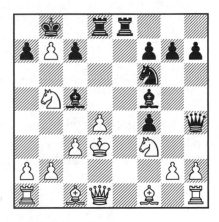

This position is white-hot! Black has sacrificed a piece for an attack right in the opening, and now White must decide where to go with his king.

13.♔c4!

This courageous move is best. After the normal 13.♔d2 ♛f2+ 14.♗e2 ♞e4+ 15.♔c2 ♞g3+! (unclear complications come after 15...♞g5+ 16.♔b3 ♜xe2 17.♞xg5! ♗c2+ 18.♕xc2 ♜xc2 19.♞e4 ♛e2 20.♞xc5 ♜xc1 21.♞xc7, where White is risking nothing) 16.♔b3 ♞xe2 17.♕f1 ♗e6+ 18.c4 (18.♔a4 would be met by 18...♞xc3+ 19.bxc3 ♛c2+, winning) 18...♗xd4, when Black stands to win, according to *Fritz 12*.

13...♗e6+ 14.♔xc5 a5

All variations beginning with 14...♘e4+ end in White's favor: 15.♔b4 ♕e7+ 16.♔a5 a6 17.♗d3 axb5 (nor does 17...♘f2 18.♕e2 ♘xh1 save Black: here 19.♗xf4 is enough to win *[although we much prefer the variation with a braver king: 19.♔xa6 g5 20.♗xf4 gxf4 21.♖xh1 ♖d6+ 22.♔a5 ♖b6 23.♕e5 ♔xb7 24.♕c5, when White should win]* 19...axb5 20.♗xb5) 18.♗xe4 ♕d6 (18...c6 looks quite dangerous at first sight; but here, too, White coolly defends his king and assures himself the win, although it wouldn't be simple: 19.♗xc6 ♕c7+ 20.♔b4 ♕xc6 21.♗xf4+ ♔xb7 22.♕d3 *[22.♘d2 or 22.b3 are alternatives]* 22...♗c4 *[White wins after 22...♖a8 23.♕xb5+ ♕xb5 24.♔xb5 ♖a6 25.d5]* 23.♕f5 ♕a6 24.a4 ♖e2 25.axb5, and Black's active position is discombobulated. The simple 25.b3 wins, too.) 19.♗xf4 ♕xf4 20.♗c6 ♕d6 21.♔xb5 (21. d5 ♗xd5 22.♕xd5 ♕xd5 23.♗xd5 ♖xd5 is also enough for White to win).

15.♘xc7! ♕h5+ 16.♘e5!

This looks like a deeply calculated combination involving a queen sacrifice. 16.d5 ♔xc7 17.♗xf4+ (17.c4) would be bad in view of 17...♔xb7 18.♕b3+ (18.c4 ♗xd5) 18...♔a8, and Black wins.

16...♘d7+

Both 16...♔xc7 17.♕xh5 ♖d5+ 18.♔c4 ♖xe5+ 19.♔d3 ♖xh5 20.♗xf4+, and 16...♕xd1 17.♘c6+ lose for Black.

17.♔b5 ♕xd1 18.♗xf4

White has carried out his attack beautifully up to this point, but here he stumbles. It's a pity, but Shtel throws away a spectacular victory in which the main role was played by the king! The win could have been had by 18.♘d7+ ♖xd7 (if 18...♔xb7, then according to *Fritz* 12 White has enough to win after 19.♘c5+ ♔a7 20.♘xe8 ♖xe8 21.♔xa5, although the actual victory would require pinpoint accuracy) 19.♗xf4 ♕xa1 20.♔b6!!, and the king himself concludes the attack:

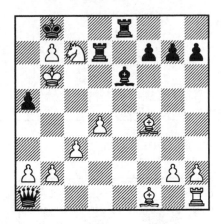

18...♕xa1 19.♔a6 ♘xe5 20.♘xe8 f6?

Returning the favor. Black wins after 20...♖d5 21.♗c4 ♕xh1 22.♗xd5 ♕f1+. Now White can carry out his attack with reduced forces. True, it's enough only to draw.

21.dxe5 f5 22.♗e3 ♖xe8 23.♗b5 ♕xh1 24.♗a7+ ♔c7 25.♗c5 ♖d8??

A blunder: the draw could be had with either 25...♗c8 or 25...♖c8.

26.♔a7!

The relentless king!

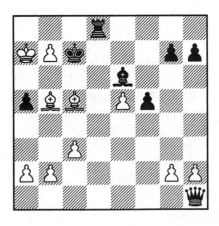

A pretty picture!

1-0

4. E. Mortensen – J. Tisdall

Gausdal 1982

With Black's last two moves, his major pieces drove into the first rank, the idea being to extract White's king. Now see how White's king, while escaping from them, also helps his own forces to weave a mating net around the opposing king.

43.♔g3!

For this example, the white king's move combines two powerful ideas: defense and attack. According to Steinitz, the king is capable of solving its own problems: at the same time, it becomes a fully effective participant in a mating attack on the opponent. Black's chief problem is not just his king, but also the poor coordination of his pieces.

43...♖h1

43...♖g1 doesn't save him: 44.♖h4+ ♔g7 (on 44...♔g6, 45.♗d3 would follow) 45.♖e4 b5 46.♖e7+ ♔g6 47.♗d3 ♖d1 48.♗e4, and White is winning.

44.♖e4

It's not clear whether White wins in the line 44.♖h4+ ♔g6 45.♗d3 ♕c3 46.♖f3+ ♔g5 47.♖g4+ ♔h6 48.♖g6+ ♔h5 49.♖e6 ♕g7+ 50.♗g6+ ♕xg6+ 51.♖xg6 ♔xg6.

44...♔g6

The cause of Black's defeat. After 44...♖e1 45.♖h4+ ♔g6 46.♗d3 ♖e3+ 47.♖f3+ ♖xd3 48.♖g4+ ♔h6 49.♖xd3, White holds the advantage, but a lot of fight remains ahead. Now, however, all of White's pieces, including the king, work together to checkmate the black king.

45.♖fe5 ♕c3+ 46.♔h4 ♖g1 47.♖e6+ ♔h7 48.g4

48.♖e7+ ♔h8 49.♔h5! also wins: White's king completes the attack.

48...♖h1 49.♖e7+ ♔h8 50.♖e8+ ♔h7 51.♖4e7+ ♔g6 52. ♖g8+ ♔f6 53.♖e6+ ♔f7 54.♖ee8+ 1-0

5. J. Tarjan – L. Ljubojević
Jakarta 1983

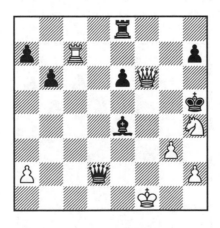

It's not hard to see from this diagram that a knock-down, drag-out battle is underway. Black's queen, along with the fantastically placed bishop, is attacking the white king; but their cooperation alone is insufficient for a mating attack. And then, out of the blue, he (Black, that is) throws his king into the assault!

30...♔g4! 31.♘f3?

Losing immediately. After the best move, 31.♔g1, the game metamorphoses into an ending: 31...♕e1+ 32.♕f1 ♕xf1+ 33.♔xf1 ♔h3, with excellent winning chances for Black.

31...♗d3+ 32.♔g1 ♕e3+ 0-1

6. I. Jelen – B. Larsen

Ljubljana/Portorož 1977

In this example, it's nice to see what kinds of problems arise when one side lures the opponent's king forward. In the attack (as in all things), we must take proper care! We have to be careful, either when attacking or when drawing his king out. In such situations, we cannot underestimate our opponent: the outcome may be regrettable. (Remember how he can turn from the hunted into the hunter!)

Up to a certain point, White was executing a consistent attack to lure the king out.

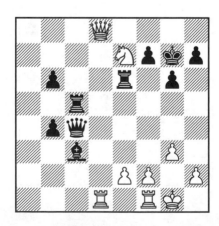

28.♕g8+?!

Fritz 12 says 28.♖d7!? is stronger; then Black would sacrifice the exchange to bring the game into a quiet line with better prospects: 28...♖xe7 29.♕xe7 ♗f6∓; on 28.e3, 28...♖xe7 also gives Black the better game. In either case, Black's advanced passed pawn guarantees him superior play.

28...♔f6

Exactly here, else 29.♕f8+ with a very dangerous attack.

29.♕h8+

Yet another computer variation underlines the fact that Black holds the upper hand despite his king's placement: 29.♕d8 ♕e4! 30.♖d3 (the discovered check 30.♘d5+ would shoot a blank: after 30...♔g7, Black completely consolidates his forces with a large advantage) 30...♖xe7! 31.♖f3+ ♔g7 32.♖e3 ♕xe3! 33.fxe3 ♖ce5, and it's not hard to see that Black's centralized – and, more importantly, beautifully coordinated – pieces can forge ahead to make good on their great advantage; whereas White, even though he is the one with the queen, has no counterplay whatever and is doomed to waiting passively.

29...♔g5 30.♕f8

Further demonstration of our theme is provided by the computer variation 30.♕d8 ♗f6! 31.♕d2+ ♔h5! 32.♘d5 (32.♘g8 ♗g7!? *[32... g5∓]*) 32...g5, with the better prospects despite his far-advanced king. We can see that up to this point the king has followed Steinitz's dictum, solving its own problems. We would like to show our hero (the king) after the move 32...♗g7 from the preceding variation:

(see diagram next page)

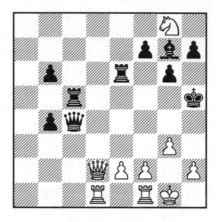

Black has the better of it here. We believe that this is an instructive position, and hope very much that the brave king will, in the future, become a more familiar sight for us.

30...♖xe2 31.♘g8

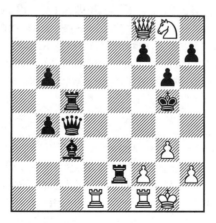

Here, too, we would like you to focus on an important moment. Black bypassed the strongest continuation, 31...♔g4!!, and instead played

31...h5??

Even *Fritz* 12 chooses 31...♔g4!!, supporting it with the following variations:

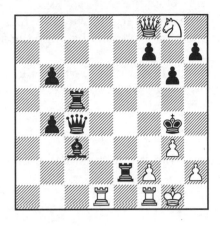

32.♖d7

Forcing variations show that Black must win after 32.♘h6+ ♔h3 33.♘xf7 ♕g4 34.♖d3 ♗e1 35.♕a8 ♗xf2+ 36.♖xf2 ♖xf2 (or 36...♖e1+ 37.♖f1 ♖xf1+ 38.♔xf1 ♖f5+) 37.♔xf2 ♖f5+ 38.♔g1 (38.♖f3 b3−+ *[or 38...♔xh2])* 38...♕e2 39.g4+ ♕xd3 40.♕g2+ ♔h4 41.gxf5 ♕b1+ 42.♔f2 (42.♕f1 ♕xf1+ 43.♔xf1 b3) 42...♕xf5+.

32...♔h3!:

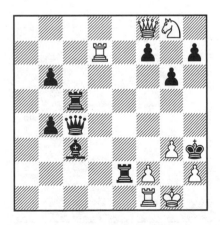

33.♖xf7 ♕e4 34.♖xh7+ ♖h5 35.♕c8+ ♕e6 36.♖xh5+ gxh5 37.♕d8 (37.♕xe6+ ♖xe6) 37...♖e4, and Black wins calmly after the likely queen trade: 38.♕d1 (or 38.♕d3 ♖d4 39.♕f3 ♕d5) 38...♖e5 39.♕f3 (39.♕d8 ♕c4! 40.♕d7+ ♔g4 also favors Black) 39...♕d5.

Once again we are witness to the way in which the king, once lured out into the open, may actually become the aggressor!

But now let us return to our game, where Black's king still has not said its final word:

32.♘h6

The winning move – but White must still play accurately all the way to the end.

32...♗d2 33.♘xf7+

Simpler winning lines are 33.♕h8, or 33.♕g7 h4 34.f4+ ♗xf4 35.♖xf4.

33...♔g4 34.♖xd2?

Apparently a miscalculation. After 34.♕d8 ♕xf7 35.h3+ ♔f5 36.♕d3+, White is on his way to winning.

34...♖xd2 35.f3+ ♔h3! 36.♕c8+ ♕g4! 37.♘g5+!

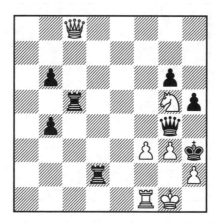

I might suggest that White placed great stock in this move; but alas, it's only good enough for a draw because of the aggressive black king, which supports the rook's bid for perpetual check.

37...♖xg5 38.fxg4 ♖g2+ 39.♔h1 ♖c5

The Danish grandmaster was famous for his knightly, uncompromising character! He passes on forcing the draw and instead sets a trap, which his opponent falls into.

40.♕d8??

Ruins the game. He could have gotten the draw with 40.♕e6 or 40.♕d7.

40...♖xh2+ 41.♔g1 g5!

Strangely enough, White no longer has any way to save himself.

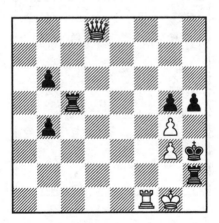

As we said before, you have to be careful when the enemy king stands so close to your own.

42.♖b1 0-1

Black also wins after 42.♕h8 ♖cc2 43.♕xh5+ ♔xg3 44.♖b1 ♖xh5 45.gxh5 ♖c6; and 42.♕e8 would lead to the same thing.

The game might continue as follows: 42...♖cc2 43.♕d5 ♖cg2+ 44.♕xg2+ ♖xg2+ 45.♔f1 hxg4 46.♖xb4 ♖xg3 47.♖xb6 ♖a3, when Black has a winning position.

With the legendary Dane, jokes can become drama!

7. G. Gajewski – L. Trent

Chalkidiki 2003

In this example Black, after winning the knight, forces White to extract Black's own king. Before launching the decisive attack, Black must calculate carefully, for his king has to undertake a dangerous journey.

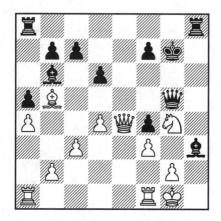

24...f5!?

For the sake of accuracy, it should be noted that Black would have won spectacularly with the unexpected combination 24... ♗xg2! 25.♔xg2 ♖h2+!!.

25.♕e6 fxg4 26.♕d7+ ♔h6

Watch and enjoy – *Fritz* offers the following as the best way to continue: 26...♔f6!!:

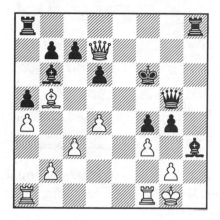

The king solves its own problems! It finds safe haven among its own pieces. And the bishop, under attack in the corner of the board at h3 (see Black's move 27), also plays an important defensive role. Now, on 27.♖ae1 gxf3 28.♕e7+ ♔g6 29.♗d3+ ♔h5 30.♕xg5+ ♔xg5 31.gxh3 ♖xh3; or 27.♗c4 ♖af8 28.♖ae1 gxf3 29.♕e7+ ♔g6 30.♕xg5+ ♔xg5 31.gxh3 ♖xh3, Black keeps his extra material, although it won't be that easy to win. Black's last move is a more natural one; but with exact play it leads to equality – even though for a time, it's a pitched battle!

27.♖ae1 ♖ag8 28.♖e6+

And here White could have played a bit more strongly: 28.♖e7! ♖g7 29.♖xg7 ♕xg7 30.gxh3 gxh3+ 31.♕xg7+ ♔xg7, with hopes of achieving full equality.

28...♔h5 29.♖e7

The decisive mistake! The instructive variation 29.fxg4+ ♗xg4 30.♕f7+ ♔h4, and now 31.♔f2!!, is just like the ones in Teichmann–Allies (Game 1), Portisch–Benjamin (Game 10), etc. The king meets its opposite number at the entrance to its residence, and bars the door:

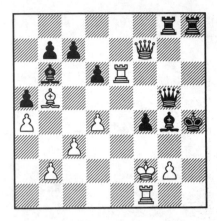

After the forced 31...♗h3 32.gxh3 ♖g7, it's equal. Once again, we see how dangerous the king (the black king, in this case) can be. But now, there followed:

29...♔h4! 30.♖h7+ ♔g3

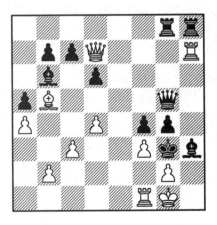

Once more (how many times have we seen this!), the king gets right in the face of its opposite number, setting insoluble problems.

31.♕e6 ♕e5!

A brilliant refutation!

32.♕xe5 dxe5 33.♖xh8 ♖xh8 0-1

Changing Roles... and Voices

8. B. Spassky – M. Tal

USSR Chp, Riga 1958

This final-round game between two future world champions had enormous significance for the prize distribution in the Soviet Championship. If Boris Spassky won the game, then Tigran Petrosian (also a future world champion) would become USSR Champion. In case of a draw, the title of Champion would be split between Petrosian and Mikhail Tal, while Spassky would get a ticket to the Interzonal tournament. In other words, the tension was exceptionally high here. And up to a certain point, Spassky got very close to his goal.

But we should really see how it all turned out.

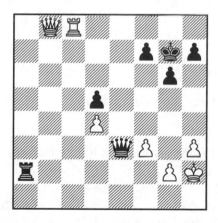

It's the accepted way of thinking – and one that I myself subscribe to – that having "queen plus rook" in any position, plus the attack, is not really an endgame, as middlegame elements predominate. So we've decided to include a few examples of this theme.

39.♖g8+ ♔f6

It probably was time pressure that prevented Tal from finding the best continuation and drawing the game with 39...♔h6 40.♕f8+

♔h5 41.♕xf7 ♖xg2+. But, as the Russians say, "there'd be no good luck, if bad luck didn't help out." Spassky now obtains winning chances, and basically starts squeezing out the win.

40.♕d6+ ♕e6 41.♕f4+ ♕f5 42.♕d6+ ♕e6 43.♕g3 ♕e3 44.h4 ♖e2

He might also have brought his rook up to defend the sixth rank with 44...♖a6.

45.♕d6+ ♕e6 46.♕f4+ ♕f5?!

A natural move which many would have made in Black's place, for 46...♔e7 47.♕c7+ ♔f6 48.♕d8+ ♕e7 49.♕xd5 looks pretty risky – although the standard 49...♖xg2+ would have led to perpetual check in that case. Incidentally, on move 47 White could have tried 47.h5, with some initiative.

Now White's threats grow more dangerous.

47.♕h6 ♔e7 48.♕f8+

A solid move. The following variations, courtesy of *Fritz* 12, look more interesting:

48.♖h8 ♔f6! (White wins in study-like fashion after 48...♕xf3? 49.♕f8+ ♔f6 50.♕d8+ ♔f5 51.♕g5+ ♔e4 *[51...♔e6 52.♖e8+]* 52.♕e7+ ♔xd4 53.♕a7+ ♔e5 54.♖e8+ ♔f6 55.♕a6+) 49.♖xh7 ♔e7! 50.♔g3 ♕f6 (the more active 50...♕c2 also loses after 51.♕f4 ♖xg2+ 52.♔h3 ♖h2+ 53.♕xh2 ♕c8+ 54.♔g2 *[White also wins after 54.♔g3 ♕c7 55.f4 ♕c3+ 56.♔g4 ♕c8+ 57.♔g5 ♕f5+ 58.♔h6]* 54...♕c2+ 55.♔h1 ♕d1+ 56.♕g1 ♕xf3+ 57.♔h2) 51.♕c1 ♔f8 52.♕c8+ ♖e8 53.♕g4 ♕d6+ 54.♔h3 ♔g8 55.♖h5, and White's inconveniently placed rook gives Black decent equalizing chances.

I hope the analysis of these continuations improves our understanding of king play. Observe how, depending on circumstances, either the king can resolve its own problems in Steinitz fashion, or its own pieces might come to its aid.

48...♔f6 49.♕g7+ ♔e7 50.♖a8 ♕d7 51.♕f8+ ♔f6 52.♖a6+

A different check would have produced a most amusing situation, with 52.♕h8+ ♔f5 53.♖a6 ♕c7+ 54.♔h3 ♔f4!!, and the king finds safe haven behind its rook (see Chapter 3).

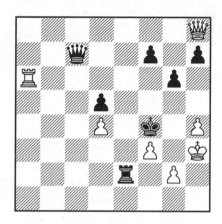

Now White cleverly weaves a mating net around the black king. It must be acknowledged that while Black's position is not at all hopeless, it is a very difficult one to play. And in fact, there's a kind of position that just makes one commit errors.

52...♖e6 53.♕h8+ ♔e7 54.♖a8 ♖e1 55.♔g3 h5 56.♔f2 ♖e6 57.♖c8 ♖d6

And here it is! As it turns out, the rook would have been better off on a different square – 57...♖b6, trying to hold a defensive position by leaving the d6 square open for the queen. Getting a queen trade would be a decent basis for achieving the draw: 57...♖b6 58.♕f8+ ♔f6 59.g4 ♖b2+ 60.♔g3 ♖b6.

58.♕f8+ ♔f6

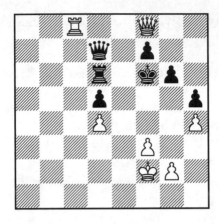

It's decision time!

59.罝e8

Instead of this healthy, sound move, White could have wrapped up the game in his favor by playing 59.g4! hxg4 60.fxg4 罝e6 61.罝c3! 罝e4 62.罝f3+ 含e6 63.g5! 豐e7 64.豐c8+ 含d6 65.豐c5+ 含d7 66.豐xd5+ 含e8, when the simplest win is the exchanging combination 67.豐xe4 豐xe4 68.罝e3!. We find the computer's variation, 67.豐a8+ 含d7 68.罝a3!, amusing as well: after 68...罝f4+ or 68...罝e2+, Black has no more checks. And that means it's hopeless for him.

59...罝e6 60.豐h8+ 含f5 61.豐h6!

The rook cannot be taken because of mate in 2.

61...含f6 62.豐h8+

Serious attention should be given to 62.罝g8! 含e7 63.豐g5+ 罝f6 64.罝a8, maintaining the initiative, when Black would have to act very incisively so as not to find himself in a hopeless situation. He might have to play 64...豐c7 here, with the idea of meeting 65.豐xd5 by checking White's king with the objective of trading off the queens and getting a draw in a pawn-down rook ending: 65...豐c2+ 66.含g1 (66.含g3 豐c7+ 67.含h3 豐d7+) 66...豐c1+ 67.含h2 豐c7+ 68.含h3 豐d7+

69.♕xd7+ ♔xd7. Please note, throughout this portion of the game, how White's pieces approach, then move away from, the black king, depending on what they need to achieve. Now White's initiative has disappeared, and the game is even. For a clear draw, White only has to trade rooks on the next move.

62...♔f5 63.♖d8 ♕c6

Why not something a bit more active like 63...♕b5, when the black queen stands ready to give perpetual check?

64.♖c8

White's job would be simpler after 64.♕f8, when it's a draw after 64...♕c2+ 65.♔g3 ♕c7+ 66.♔h3 ♖e1 67.♖xd5+ ♔e6 68.♕e8+ ♔xd5 69.♕xe1 ♔xd4. It looks as though it was at precisely this moment that Spassky saw he had lost his advantage; but he kept playing aggressively, out of inertia.

64...♕a6 65.♔g3?

The king wants to leave the danger zone, but it's too soon for that. Now he comes under fire from the opposite direction. He could have gotten the draw with the vigorous 65.♕d8; but now the initiative switches over to Black.

We are seeing a moment when the attacking side, in luring away the king, underestimates its hidden possibilities. Now it is the black king that menaces its opponent.

65...♕d6+ 66.♔h3 ♖e1 67.g3?

It was hard to do, but he had to take his last opportunity and play 67.g4+ hxg4 68.fxg4+ ♔f4 69.♖c3!?, and here Black can choose between 69...♖e3+ or 69...♔e4, with chances to play for the win.

67...♖g1

67...♕a6! ends the game at once.

68.f4 ♖e1 69.♖c2

69.♖e8 is necessary; although after 69...♖xe8 70.♕xe8 ♕e6, White faces an uphill battle for the draw.

69...♕e6 70.♖f2

This loses right away. He has to try his luck with 70.♕c8 ♕xc8 71.♖xc8 ♖e4.

70...♖h1+ 71.♔g2 ♕e4+ 72.♖f3 ♔g4 73.♕c8+ f5 0-1

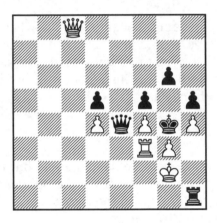

The reader will probably have guessed by now why we spoke of "changing roles" in the title to this section. While assailing his opponent's king, White overstepped the well-known bounds of caution that we wrote about earlier. And the king, formerly the hunted, became the hunter, participating in a mating attack.

And what did we have in mind when speaking of a "change in voice"? Interesting story. Nikolai Krogius, a well-known Russian grandmaster (and also a psychologist), wrote that Spassky, realizing that he had lost the advantage, offered a draw. At first, Tal was about to agree; but then he decided to refuse. (You should also know that at that point the position was equal, and a draw would make Tal USSR Champion along with Petrosian; also, he would have to slog through a difficult defense for the adjournment.) In short, everything indicated he should take the draw. And yet, Tal refused!

It turned out that, as he offered the draw, Spassky's voice quavered! Tal noticed this subtlety. He saw that his opponent had lost his nerve – so he decided to play on!

A most instructive moment from a psychological angle! Tal's decision would have delighted the heart of our second world champion, Emanuel Lasker, who was a great specialist in the field of chess psychology.

9. L. Aronian – E. Danielian

Yerevan 1998

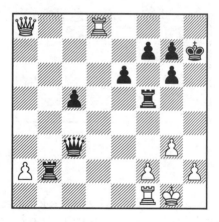

This game between a pair of gifted Armenian players, Levon Aronian and Elina Danielian, took place when they were still very young.

Black holds an unquestionable edge. First, using simple moves, she gets her king out of the danger zone.

28...g5 29.♖h8+ ♔g6 30.h4 ♖bxf2 31.h5+ ♔f6 32.♕d8+ ♔e5 33.♕b8+ ♔e4 34.♕b1+ ♖c2 35.♖e1+ ♔f3

Black's king has moved right up to White's, and now seriously threatens mate.

36.♖d8 ♔g4 37.♕d1+ ♔h3

Attacking, first from the left, then from the right!

38.♖d3 ♖g2+ 39.♔h1 ♖h2+ 40.♔g1 ♕b2 41.g4+ ♔h4

The eight-move journey has ended successfully. Notice how comfortable the black king is in the diagram.

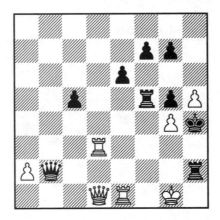

0-1

Now let us move on to games where the king gets aggressive in more complex positions. Here, as a rule, the king provides both attack and defense.

10. L. Portisch – J. Benjamin

Szirak 1987

Black has just given discovered check. So where should we go with the king? Backwards, to a safer place? Of course not – instead, we attack: to g6! Wouldn't you say that this is like Game 1 by Teichmann? Black has the same kingside pawn structure, with a weak g6 square; and for White there's the same active tandem of queen-plus-knight. And now – the same shockingly aggressive king!

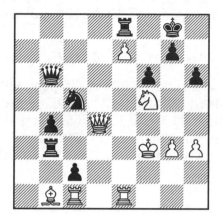

44.♔g4!

Fritz 12 correctly assesses 44.♔g2 cxb1♕ 45.♖xb1 ♕c6+ 46.♔g1 ♘e6 in Black's favor.

44...♕c6

If 44...cxb1♕, then 45.♕d5+ and Black has to be careful, as White threatens a deadly incursion at f7. Only 45...♘e6!! saves him: on 46.♖xb1 ♖xb1 47.♖xe6, we have 47...♖d1!! with a likely draw after 48.♕e4 ♕c5 49.♘xh6+ ♔h8 50.♘f7+. If White gives the alternative check 45.♕c4+, then Black replies 45...♘e6!! 46.♖xb1 ♖xb1 47.♖xe6, and now the saving move is 47...♖c1!!. This variation demonstrates once again the complex tasks Black has to solve after Portisch brings his king forward into the attack.

45.♔h5 cxb1♕ 46.♖xb1 ♕f3+?

An error in calculation: Black could not stand the tension. In fact, after 46...♔h7!! the king attacks become mutual. (By the way, notice that the same move, ...♚h7, could also have occurred in Teichmann's game.)

For example, 47.♕g4 ♕f3! when White has to be on his toes:

a) 48.♕xf3? ♖xf3 49.♘d6 g6+ 50.♚h4 h5, and here we like Black's chances better;

b) 48.♖xb3? g6 49.♚h4 ♕xb3, and Black's win is not so far away;

c) Only 48.♖bd1! promises White equal chances: 48...g6+ 49.♚h4 g5+ 50.♚h5 ♕xg4+ 51.hxg4 (51.♚xg4 is dubious because of 51...♚g6 52.h4 h5+ 53.♚h3 ♘d3 54.♖f1 ♘f4+ 55.♚h2 ♚xf5 56.gxf4 ♖b2+ 57.♚g1 gxf4, when Black should win) 51...♖b2 52.♖d8 ♖h2+ (52...♘d3?? 53.♖h1, and White wins) 53.♘h4 ♘d3 54.♖f1! gxh4 55.gxh4 ♖xe7 56.♖xd3, with a likely draw.

But now, White's dream comes true: his king gets to g6, where he unilaterally attacks his opposite number.

47.♚g6!

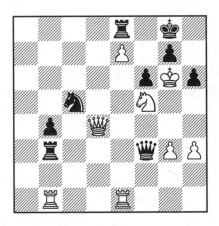

47...♖d3 48.♕xc5 ♖d5 49.♖f1!

Black apparently overlooked this move when playing 46...♕f3+. White avoids the trap and gets a winning game. Both 49.♕c8??

♕xg3+ 50.♘xg3 ♖g5# and 49.♕c2?? ♕xg3+ 50.♘xg3 ♖g5# end in disaster.

49...♖xf5 50.♕xf5 ♕xg3+ 51.♔h5 ♖xe7 52.♖g1 ♕c3 53.♖bc1 ♖e5 54.♖xc3 ♖xf5+ 55.♔g6 1-0

White handled his king better than his opponent did, and that decided the outcome. There was a reason GM Portisch was one of the top chessplayers on the planet.

Still another Nigel Short victory – this one over the great Garry Kasparov! Kasparov is way ahead in their individual encounters; but in this game, the Englishman flung his king into the attack, and his brave sortie proved decisive. The World Champion put up what resistance he could, but was helpless in the end.

Our advice to you is: make use of any chance that may turn up! Even against the World Champion...

11. G. Kasparov – N. Short

London 1987

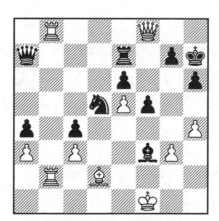

This was a rapid game, played at 25 minutes apiece. Apparently time pressure was a factor here, which is why the World Champion overlooked the king march.

Black had planned to march his king to g3, creating mating threats. Kasparov put a stop to this aggressive-minded king, but he lost because of other, no less dangerous threats:

45...♔g6 46.♗c1

Fatal dithering.

Necessary was 46.♖e8!, attacking the black rook that defends the g7-pawn, and thus holding back the king's march. 46...♕d7 would then lead to unclear play with what appear to be equal chances, for instance 47.♖xe7 (an alternative continuation would be 47.♖d8, striving for equality) 47...♘xe7 48.♔g1, when it's hard for either side to upset the balance.

46...♔h5 47.♖a8

Now 47.♖e8 is no longer sufficient, due to 47...♘e3+ 48.♗xe3 ♕xe3 49.♕xe7 (Black wins after 49.♖xe7 ♗e4 50.♕b8 ♔g4, bringing up the king for the decisive attack – although 50...♕f3+ 51.♔e1 ♕xg3+ also wins) 49...♗e4! and, little by little, Black grinds out the win: 50.g4+!? fxg4 51.♕f7+ ♔g6 52.♕f2 ♕c1+ 53.♕e1 ♕xb2 54.♖xe6 ♗d3+ 55.♔g1 g3 56.♕xg3 ♕c1+ 57.♔f2 ♕d2+ 58.♔g1 ♕d1+ 59.♔h2 ♗e4 60.♕g1 ♕d2+ 61.♔g3 ♕xc3+ 62.♔h2 ♕d2+ 63.♔g3 ♕d3+ 64.♔h2 ♕e2+.

Black also wins if White refrains from capturing the knight: 48.♔f2 ♘g4+ 49.♔xf3 (49.♔f1 ♖d7!? *[49...♕a5 is also winning]* 50.♖d8 ♖b7! 51.♖d4 ♖xb2 52.♕e8+ g6 53.♗xb2 ♕b7) 49...♕g1 50.♔e2 ♕f2+ 51.♔d1 ♕f1+ 52.♔d2 ♖d7+ 53.♕d6 ♖xd6+ 54.exd6 ♘f2.

47...♕c5

Black would have won more confidently after 47...♘e3+ 48.♗xe3 ♕xe3 49.♖ab8 ♗e4 50.♕xe7 ♕f3+ 51.♔g1 ♕xg3+ 52.♔f1 ♗d3+ 53.♖e2 ♕f3+ 54.♔g1 ♕xe2 55.♕xg7 ♗e4.

48.♖c8

If he plays 48.♖e8 again, then after 48...♘e3+ (48...♗e4 looks strong, too) 49.♗xe3 ♕xe3 we get the same variations we saw in the note to White's move 47.

48...♕xa3 49.g4+ ♗xg4 50.♖xc4 ♕a1 0-1

In the following game, the legendary Georgian and future 5-time Women's World Champion, Nona Gaprindashvili, had the black pieces.

12. M. Lazarević – N. Gaprindashvili

Vrnjačka Banja 1961

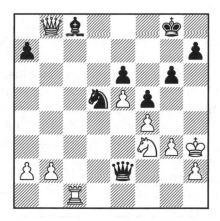

In the diagram, Black's position is difficult if not hopeless, so she makes the only practical decision.

27...♔g7

This is not merely running away from the enemy army – as you will soon discover. In any case, after 27...♘xf4+?! 28.♔h4 ♔g7 29.♖c7+ ♔h6 30.♖xh7+ ♔xh7 31.♔g5! (see diagram), White's king decides the attack.

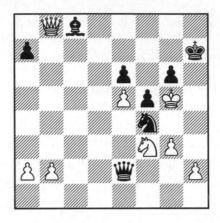

Incidentally, this is a nice example of extracting the opponent's king to one's own detriment.

28.♕xa7?

This looks like a useful move. From the a3 square, the queen protects the knight, just as it would from b3; it also eyes f8, from where it can attack Black's king. But Black plays just two king moves and the situation turns 180 degrees. Winning was 28.♕b3. Once more, we see a situation in which the attacking player fails to notice counterplay, where the lead role is played by the opposing king, and the position goes from winning to drawing. And that's not all...

28...♚h6 29.♕a3 ♚h5!

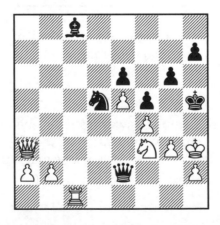

Here is that counterplay, which Lazarević clearly underestimated. Now Black is seriously playing for mate. White has to tread very carefully to avoid losing.

30.♖e1?

After the best move, 30.♖g1!, the most likely outcome is a draw; now Gaprindashvili is winning. But we can agree that it's not so easy to find a move like 30.♖g1 when time is running out.

30.♖g1! g5 31.fxg5 ♗a6 32.g4+ fxg4+ 33.♖g4 ♕f2 34.♖h4+ ♔g6 35.♖h6+ ♔g7 36.♔g4 (36.♕xa6 ♕xf3+ 37.♔h4) 36...♘e3+ (36... ♗d3) 37.♔f4 ♘g2, and it's a draw in all lines.

30...♕f2 31.♕d3 ♗a6 32.♕d1 ♘e3 0-1

13. B. Spassky – L. Polugaevsky
Moscow 1961

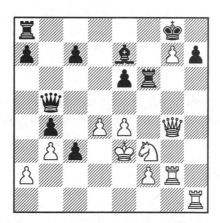

We should note that, in the very opening, Boris Spassky (later to become the tenth world champion) willingly gave up his right to castle and then advanced the most important piece right up to e3. In the diagram position, Spassky answers blow for blow, with the result that his king continues to creep into the enemy camp.

30.♖xh7

White also wins after 30.e5 ♖g6 31.♕h5 ♔f7 32.♖xg6 hxg6 33.♘g5+ ♗xg5+ 34.♕xg5. Black has nothing else but to take his last chance.

30...♖xf3+ 31.♔xf3 ♕d3+ 32.♔f4 ♗d6+ 33.♔g5 ♔xh7

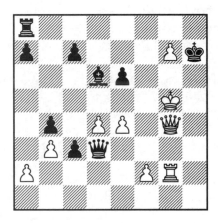

The tension reaches its peak. Had Spassky played 34.♔f6! here, bringing his king into what was certain to be a winning attack, he would have won, e.g. 34...♕xd4+ 35.♔f7. Instead, he played...

34.♔h5

...and gave his opponent some counterplay. But now the game becomes a complicated rook ending, where Black's passed pawn will be just as dangerous as White's.

34...♕b5+ 35.♔h4

It's somewhat surprising to us that Spassky prefers this quiet, clear continuation: 35.e5 ♕e8+ 36.♔h4 ♔g8 leads to head-spinning complications, more in the spirit of this future world champion. How many games he's won this way! But now the game winds up in an unusual rook ending of dynamic equality.

35...♗e7+ 36.♔h3 ♕g5! 37.♕xg5 ♗xg5 38.♖xg5 ♖d8 39.f4

39.f3 looks more compact, and safer.

39...♔g8 40.♖c5 ♖xd4 41.♖xc7 ♖xe4 42.♔g4 e5?!

This natural move leads to a draw after 43.♔f5! ♖xf4+ 44.♔g6. After the strongest move, 42...♔h7!, White faces a hard fight to make the draw. (The king move would have prevented the White king's invasion at g6.)

43.a3?

Returning the favor.

43...♖xf4+

Accurately played. It would be with interesting complexity, but Black nevertheless would have won after 43...bxa3!?, for instance 44.♔f5 (44.♔g5 exf4 45.♖xc3 ♔xg7 46.♖c7+ ♔f8 47.♔f5 ♖e1! and Black's passed pawns decide) 44...exf4!! 45.♖xc3 ♖b4 46.♖c8+ ♔xg7 47.♖c7+ ♔h6 48.♖xa7 f3 49.♖xa3 ♔h5!, and Black wins.

44.♔g5 a5 45.♔g6

After 45.axb4 axb4 46.♔g6 ♖g4+ 47.♔h6 e4!! Black wins, thanks to his passed pawns, in the ♖+♙ vs. ♙s endgame. Another way to lose is 47.♔f6 ♔h7 48.♔xe5 ♖xg7 49.♖c6 ♖g1, after which White has no way to sharpen play and Black's victory is only a matter of time, since he can gradually bring his king up for an easy win.

45...♖g4+ 46.♔f6

Nor does 46.♔h6 change things. Black wins with the "ugly" but powerful 46...bxa3, e.g. 47.♖xc3 a2 48.♖c8+ ♔f7 49.♖f8+ ♔e6 50.♖f1 e4 51.♖a1 ♔f6 52.♖f1+ ♔e5 53.♖a1 ♖g2.

The game ended with:

46...♔h7 47.g8♕+ ♔xg8 48.♔xe5 ♖g1 49.♔f6 ♖f1+ 50.♔e5 ♖b1 0-1

14. L. Psakhis – A. Vītoliņš

Frunze 1979

Latvian IM Alvis Vītoliņš was a player with a very active style. In this game against the two-time USSR Champion, Lev Psakhis, as in our previous example, not only did he get his king out of the danger zone, but he even brought it into the attack on White's king. It is true that, in contrast to the preceding example, Black stands considerably better here, and therefore his aggressive-king plan is probably the best there is in this position.

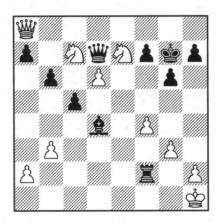

32...♔h6! 33.♘g8+

33.♕c8 ♕xc8 34.♘xc8 ♖d2 35.♘e7 ♔h5 36.h3 c4 37.bxc4 ♗c5 loses, too.

33...♔h5 34.♕d5+ ♕f5?

Black evidently overlooked White's reply. The consistent 34... ♔g4! 35.♕g5+ ♔f3 36.♕d5+ ♔e3 wins for Black – White would be unable to ward off Black's decisive threats.

(see diagram next page)

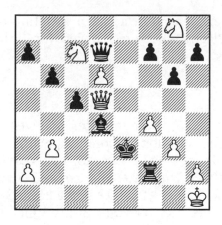

But now it's a draw:

35.h3 ♖f1+ **36.♔g2** ♖f2+ **37.♔h1** ♖f1+ **38.♔g2** ♖f2+ **39.♔h1** ½-½

15. I. Cheparinov – E. Sutovsky

Poikovsky 2013

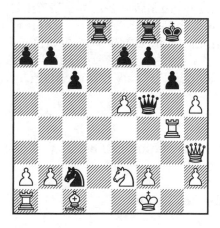

This position comes out of a sharp variation of the Grünfeld Defense, where Black has sacrificed a piece for the initiative. White plays the obvious

22.hxg6

Now after 22...fxg6, the computer believes the position is equal. Here are the variations it comes up with: 22...fxg6 23.♘f4 ♖d1+ 24.♔e2! (24.♔g2 ♕e4+ 25.f3 *[25.♔g3 ♕xe5 26.♖xg6+ ♔f7 27.♕h7+ ♔e8 28.♖e6 ♕g5+ 29.♔h3 ♖g1]* 25...♘e1+ 26.♔g3 ♖d3 27.♖xg6+ ♕xg6+) 24...♖e1+ 25.♔d2 ♖d8+ 26.♔c3 ♘xa1 27.♖xg6+ ♕xg6 28.♘xg6 ♖xc1+ 29.♔b4 ♖d4+ 30.♔a3 ♘c2+ 31.♔b3 ♘a1+; and, at the end of this beautiful variation, we get an entertaining draw!

But Black figures that he is obligated to attack the king, so he plays

22...♖d1+ 23.♔g2 ♘e1+?

Played in the same spirit – even though here, too, 23...fxg6 is better. After 24.♕b3+ ♖d5 (worse is 24...♔g7 25.♗h6+ ♔xh6 26.♕h3+ ♕h5 *[Black loses in the variation 26...♔g7 27.♖xd1 ♕xf2+ 28.♔h1]* 27.♖xg6+ ♔xg6 28.♕xh5+ ♔h5 29.♖xd1, when White has an extra pawn and real winning chances) 25.♕g3 ♘xa1 26.♘f4 ♕e4+ 27.♔h3 ♕xe5 28.♘xg6 ♕xg3+ 29.♔xg3 ♖a5 30.♘xf8+ ♔xf8, despite White's advantage, Black's hopes for salvation remain alive.

24.♔g3 ♕f3+

24...♕xe5+ won't save him, either: 25.f4 ♖d3+ 26.♔f2 ♕xe2+ 27.♔xe2 ♖h3 28.♔xe1.

25.♔h4 ♕xf2+ 26.♔g5 f6+

If 26...♘f3+, then 27.♔h6 ♕xh2 28.♕xh2 ♘xh2 29.gxf7+ ♔xf7 30.♖g7+ ♔e6 31.♖xe7+! ♔e7 32.♗g5+ ♔f7 33.e6+!, and White wins.

27.♔h6

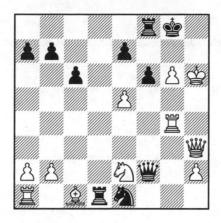

Not only has White's king found shelter, it is also ready to support a mating attack should Black continue with 27...♕xe2. Some sample variations: 28.♖e1 ♕g2 (28...♕xe4 29.♕e6+ ♔h8 30.g7#) 29.♕e6+ ♔h8 30.h4.

The game concluded with

27...f5 28.♖g3 ♕xe2 29.♔g5! ♖f7 30.gxf7+ ♔xf7 31.♕xf5+ ♔e8 32.♗f4 ♖xa1 33.e6 1-0

Chapter 2

The Active King

In this chapter we examine two situations:

1. where the king doesn't participate in an attack on the opposing king, but rather attacks the opponent's pieces;
2. where the king controls vital squares.

A. The King Attacks the Opposing Pieces

1. A. Alekhine – J.R. Capablanca

AVRO 1938

White's advantage is unquestionable. With courageous play, Alexander Alekhine, the fourth world champion, finds the shortest route to victory by immediately attacking the f3-knight's support.

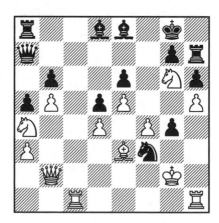

31.♔g3! ♕f7 32.♔xg4 ♘h4

32...♘g5 33.fxg5 ♕f5+ 34.♔g3 ♗xg5 35.♖cf1, with a winning position.

33.♘xh4 ♕xh5+ 34.♔g3 ♕f7 35.♘f3 1-0

2. A. Karpov – N. Krogius

Kuibyshev 1970

Future world champion Anatoly Karpov directs his king brilliantly:

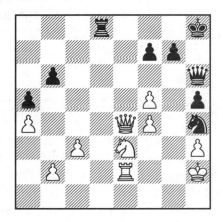

1.♔g3!! g5

Forced: on 1...♕f6, there is 2.♕e5.

2.fxg6 ♘xg6 3.♘f5 ♕f8

If 3...h4+, then 4.♔g4!.

**4.♕f3 ♔g8 5.♕xh5 ♖d3+ 6.♔g4! ♕a8 7.♘d4 ♖d1 8.♘f3!
♖d5**

8...♖f1 is met by 9.♔g3!.

9.♘g5 ♕c8+ 10.♔f3

10.♔g3, leaving the h2 square for his king, is more accurate.

10...♖f5?

Black might have put up more resistance after 10...♖d3+! 11.♖e3.

11.♕h7+ ♔f8 12.♕h6+ ♔g8 13.♘e6! 1-0

Karpov's brilliant play inspires admiration. No surprise that this event made him Russian Champion at age 19! Savor how, in this game, the twelfth world champion used not only his king, but also his queen and knight. What fantastic piece coordination on such a small part of the board! This is the first known game by Karpov where he showed an amazing feel for the masterly use of the king.

3. A. Karpov – A. Yusupov

USSR Chp, Moscow 1983

Your author, to his great pleasure, witnessed this game as a spectator. These dramatic events were followed, not just by the spectators – the participants in this USSR Championship formed a tight ring around the board where this battle was taking place. I recalled the game Karpov–Krogius 13 years earlier. Don't the motifs look familiar?

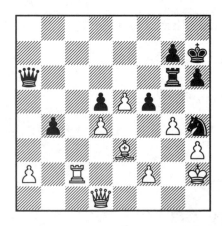

38.♔g3!

Looks risky – but White has everything worked out.

38...fxg4 39.♔xh4! gxh3

If 39...g3, then 40.fxg3 ♕a3 – and now, thanks to the twin threats of 41...b3 and 41...♕xe3, it looks like Black has sufficient counterplay. But White can play 41.♕c1!, throwing cold water on Black's attack.

40.f4! ♕e6 41.♕h5 ♕e7+ 42.♔xh3 ♕f7

Black's last hope was for a discovered attack with 42...♖g3+. But now there comes a typical Karpovian prophylactic move; and within a couple of moves, Black resigned.

43.♖h2! ♕d7+ 44.f5 1-0

4. P. Korbuzov – V. Malaniuk

Tallinn 1983

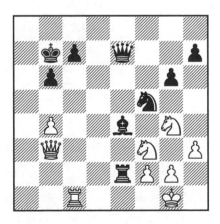

From this position, the game went...

38.♕c3 ♗xf3 39.♕xf3+ ♔b8 40.♕c3 ♖e6

...and White agreed to a draw in a better position.

Meanwhile, White could have gained a big advantage by going after Black's rook with his king: 38.♔f1!, when if 38...c6, for instance, then 39.b5! c5 and now White could pose Black a set of insoluble problems with 40.♖a1!.

5. R. Hübner – A. Beliavsky

Munich 1990

Earlier in the game, White had made a positional piece sacrifice for this powerful pin. The *dénouement* was sudden and unexpected. First, the king attacks the pinning piece:

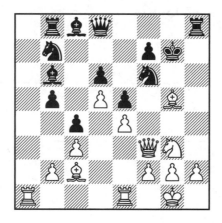

23...♔g6! 24.♘f5

White has to play something active, as otherwise there comes 24...♗g4.

24...♔xg5

Now the king removes that dangerous bishop, not fearing to lead his army into battle! The finish went:

25.♕g3+ ♘g4 26.h4+ ♔f6 27.♕xg4 ♕g8 28.♕f3 ♗xf5
(best) **29.♕xf5+ ♔e7 30.♕h3 ♕g6 31.g3 ♘c5 32.♔f1 ♕f6 0-1**

B. The King Defends His Pieces And Controls Important Squares

6. J.R. Capablanca – O. Chajes

New York 1918

One of the varieties of king activity. Here, the king does *not* attack the opponent's pieces, but controls important entry points or defends its own troops.

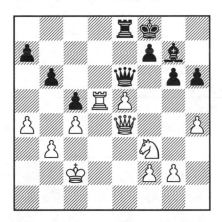

29.♔d3 ♔g8 30.♖d6 ♕c8 31.♖d5 ♕e6 32.g4 ♔f8 33.♕f4 ♔g8 34.♕e4 ♔f8 35.♔e2 ♔g8 36.♔f1 ♔f8 37.♔g2 ♔g8 38.♔g3

From here, the king controls the black queen's invasion squares.

38...♔f8 39.h5 gxh5 40.gxh5 ♕e7 41.♕f5 ♔g8 42.♖d7 ♗xe5+ 43.♔g4!

While here, His Majesty shows concern for the queen, protecting her, and rendering the bishop capture playable, when White's advantage will be decisive. 43.♔g2 ♕f6 would result in a long, drawn-out battle, in which Black would retain drawing chances.

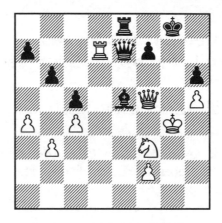

43...♕f6 44.♘xe5 ♕g7+ 45.♔f4 1-0

7. A. Petrosian – A. Beliavsky

USSR Chp, Riga 1973

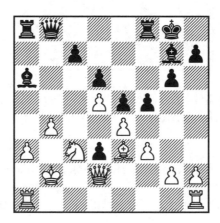

23.♔b3!

The king supports the advance of the a- and b-pawns, while simultaneously keeping the c4 square under control. It's not hard to understand why Black seeks to create counterplay.

23...♖c8 24.a4 c6 25.dxc6 ♖xc6 26.b5 d5

Trying to confuse matters. If 26...f4, then 27.♕xd3.

27.♘xd5 ♗f8

Nothing comes of the sacrifice on b5.

28.♕xd3 ♕d6 29.♔b2

Preventing the bishop sacrifice on b5. A different possibility is 29.♘f6+. Sometimes, choosing a move becomes a matter of taste.

29...♖b8 30.♖hc1

Assemble, everybody!

30...♔h8 31.♖c3

The line 31.♖xc6 ♕xc6 32.♕b3 ♗xb5 33.♘c3 is pretty entertaining: suddenly, it's Black who's suffering!

31...♗b7 32.♖ac1

32.♖b3! is possible, too. There followed:

32...fxe4 33.fxe4 ♖xc3 34.♖xc3 ♗xd5 35.♗c5 ♕f6 36.♕xd5 ♖d8 37.♕c6

37.♖f3 is strong as well.

37...♕f4 38.♗xf8 ♕xf8 39.♕c5 ♕f4 40.♕c6 ♕d2+ 41.♔a3 h5 42.♕f6+ ♔h7 43.♖c7+ ♔h6 44.♕g7+ ♔g5 45.♕xe5+ ♔h6 46.♕g7+ ♔g5 47.♖c5+ ♔h4 48.♕f6+ g5 49.♕xg5+ 1-0

8. Y. Seirawan – J. Timman

Wijk aan Zee 1980

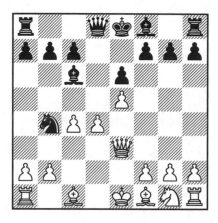

Remember how, in our youth, we dreamed about playing a knight fork? How happy we felt when we got the chance to do it! In this game between two very strong grandmasters, Black's knight is close to fulfilling our childhood dream. How does White meet this? The answer is not easy – the more so in that Black has, for the time being, a considerable edge in development.

10.♔d2!

The king takes an important square under its personal protection. This move became possible thanks to the panzer formation of white center pawns. Black cannot break through the opposing pawn chain. And White, after setting up his king on the queenside, goes about quietly completing development (10.♕c3 doesn't work because of 10...♗e4 – this is stronger than 10...♕xd4).

10...a5 11.a3 ♘a6 12.♔c2 ♕d7 13.♘f3 ♗e7 14.♗d2 0-0 15.♗c3 b5

The only way to try to stir the pot.

16.cxb5 ♗xb5 17.♗xb5 ♕xb5 18.♖hd1

A preparatory move. Preparing what? Ah – you'll see.

18...♖fd8 19.♔d2

And now the white king heads for the relative safety of the king-side – evacuation!

19...♘b4

Black tries with all his might to halt the white king's march – although 19...♘c5 was objectively stronger, e.g. 20.♔e1 ♘b3 21.♖ab1, with a minimal edge for White.

20.♕e2!

Now White's position is to be preferred.

20...♕b7 21.axb4 axb4

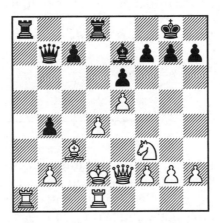

22.♔e1

And here it is: the evacuation of the king – one of our king-play methods in defense. This method will be examined in Chapter 3.

22...bxc3 23.bxc3 ♛b3 24.♛d3 ♖xa1 25.♖xa1 h6 26.♖b1 ♛a3 27.♛c4 c5 28.♔f1 ♛a8 29.h3 ♖c8 30.♛b5 cxd4 31.cxd4 ♛a2 32.♔g1

The situation has clarified: White has successfully evacuated his king and owns an extra pawn, with well-coordinated pieces; he can look forward to winning. However, with accurate play, Black has chances for salvation. Wise men will tell you, though, that bad positions often give rise to further mistakes. It's difficult to play a position where there's no clear-cut plan of action, but you have to skillfully stand in place.

32...♝g5 33.♖e1 ♝f4 34.♛d7 ♖b8

Perhaps it would be better to play 34...♛a8 right away?

35.g3 ♛a8

Now this move runs into a powerful rejoinder.

36.d5! ♖d8 37.♛c6 ♛xc6 38.dxc6 ♝g5 39.♘xg5 hxg5 40.♔g2 ♖c8 41.♖c1 f5 1-0

9. L. Psakhis – M. Hebden

Chicago 1983

In the diagram below, White has nailed Black down to defending the f7-pawn, but making good on his own extra pawn will not be easy. Grandmaster Lev Psakhis, a two-time USSR Champion, is famed for his king play, and with good reason! He sends his most important piece over to the queenside, threatening trades on f7 in order to turn the game into a winning pawn ending. A great idea!

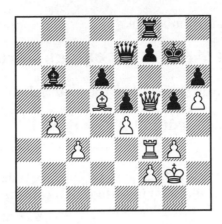

43.♔f1! ♗a7 44.♔e2 ♗b6 45.♔d3 ♗a7 46.♔c4 ♕c7+ 47.♔b3 ♕e7 48.g4!

Fixing the kingside pawns.

48...♗b6 49.♔c4 ♗a7 50.♔b5!

There is a beautiful variation here: 50...♖b8+ 51.♔a6!!:

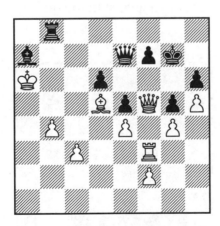

and if 51...♖b6+, then 52.♔a5 and it's time for Black to resign.

50...♕e8+ 51.♗c6 ♕d8 52.♔c4 ♕e7 53.♕d7

Forcing a winning endgame.

53...♕e6+ 54.♕xe6 fxe6 55.♖xf8 ♔xf8 56.♔b5 ♔e7 57.♔a6

The tempo is worth more than the material.

57...♗xf2 58.c4 ♔d8 59.♔b7 ♗e1 60.b5 ♗f2 61.b6 ♗d4 62.♗a4 d5

This counterplay is insufficient. If 62...♗c5, then 63.♗b5 – *Zugzwang!* This lets the white king attack and capture Black's central pawns unhindered.

63.cxd5 exd5 64.exd5 e4 65.♔c6 ♔c8 66.d6 e3 67.♗b5 ♗f6 68.♗a6+ ♔b8 69.♔d7 1-0

10. A. Krechetov – M. Khachian

USA 2003

The following position is quite unique: you don't usually see the king taking up such a startling post in the middle of the opponent's camp.

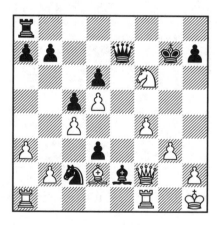

23...♔xf6! 24.♗c3+ ♔f5!!

How unique is that! Usually, this is a nice place for a knight – occasionally, a queen or a bishop – blockading the f4-pawn. Once again, this begs for a diagram. Enjoy!

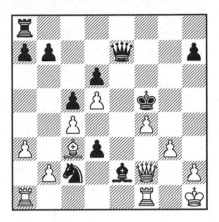

This has become possible because the kingside light squares are under Black's total control.

25.h3 h5!

Just like the classics! The pawn secures the king's powerful position against the threat of 26.g4+.

26.♖g1

26.♖ae1 is better.

26...♘xa1 27.♖xa1 ♛e4+ 28.♔h2 ♛xc4 29.♖e1 ♖g8 30. ♛e3?

This loses. He had to sharpen the game with 30.♖xe2! dxe2 31.♛f3, with complex play. *Fritz* 12 suggests that Black queen his e-pawn here, with the better chances.

30...♛e4 31.♛f2 b6 32.♗d2 a5 33.a4 ♖g6 34.♖g1 ♛f3 35.♛e1 ♔e4!

Invasion!

36.♕c1 ♔xd5 37.♕c3 h4 38.♗e1 ♗f1 39.♕b3+ ♔c6 40.♕f7 hxg3+ 41.♗xg3 ♕e2+ 42.♔h1 ♖h6 0-1

A brilliant creative achievement by the Armenian master who was GM Levon Aronian's first trainer.

11. A. Karpov – J. Nunn

London 1982

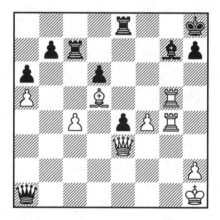

The time for decisive action has come; Karpov mobilizes all of his forces on the kingside. And this doesn't exclude his king, which is supporting its major pieces from behind.

39.♔g2 ♕b2+

If 39...♕xa5, then White wins beautifully with 40.♕d4!.

40.♔h3 ♖ce7 41.f5 ♕f6 42.♖h5 ♖f8 43.♖gh4

Karpov's methodical play induces the weakening of the g6 square.

43....h6 44.♖g4 ♖e5 45.♖gg5! ♖c8 46.♔g4!

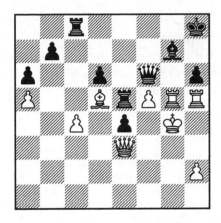

Protecting the h5-rook. Now he threatens 47.♖g6 which, if played immediately, would lose to 46...♕xg6. The king move also avoids any unpleasantness along the third rank – for example, after an exchange sacrifice with ...♖xd5.

46...♔h7

After 46...♖xd5, White wins simply with 47.cxd5 ♖c3 48.♕xe4.

47.♖g6 ♕f8 48.♕g5!

A pretty picture!

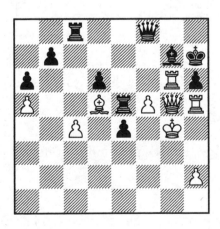

Look at White's major pieces, clustered around the white king and f5-pawn. In the world of gymnastics, there's "Albert Azarian's cross" (a three-time Olympic gymnastics champion) on the rings *[known in the West as the "iron cross" – Tr.]*. The "Anatoly Karpov cross" is not one bit inferior to that!

The finish was:

48...♕xf5+ 49.♕xf5 ♖xf5 50.♖xg7+ ♔xg7 51.♖xf5 1-0

12. F. Caruana – Wang Hao

Bucharest 2013

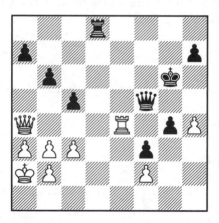

The ♕+♖ combination lends the position a little bite. True, Black's king is not under attack here as it was in Spassky–Tal.

34...♔h5 35.♖e1

After 35.♖f4 ♕g6, Black's position is preferable.

35...h6

He could have protected the pawn with 35...♖d7.

36.♕xa7 g3 37.fxg3?

Grandmaster Dorian Rozogenko correctly believes that White overlooked a chance to draw the game here: 37.♕e7 gxf2 38.♖e5 ♕xe5 39.♕xe5+ ♔g4 40.♕e4+ ♔g3 41.♕g6+ ♔h2 42.♕c2 ♔g1 43.♕g6+.

37...f2 38.♖f1 ♔g4 39.♕g7+ ♔f3

Towards the center! Because, in certain circumstances, along with anything else, the king could attack its white colleague. 39... ♔h3 is also quite playable.

40.g4 ♕f4 41.♕b7+ ♔e2 42.♖b1 ♖d3

42...f1♕! is more in accordance with our theme: 43.♕e7+ ♔d2 44.♕xd8+ ♔c2 45.♖xf1 ♕xf1, with unavoidable mate (aggressive king!). Our last position deserves a diagram:

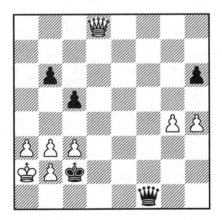

43.♕g2

Here again, we agree with GM Rogozenko, who considers 43.♕xb6 the most stubborn reply.

After 43...f1♕ 44.♖xf1, Wang Hao would still have had to find 44...♕xf1! (44...♔xf1? leads to an unclear position after 45.♕xc5

♕xg4 46.♕f8+ ♔e2 47.♕xh6, when Black would hardly be able to win) 45.♕xc5 ♔d2! 46.a4 ♔c2, with strong winning chances.

After the game move, however, Black has an easy win.

43...♖d1 44.♖xd1 ♔xd1 45.♕f1+ ♔d2 46.g5 hxg5 47.hxg5 ♕g3 48.♕b5 ♕d3 0-1

There are more than enough examples of the king's actively escorting its passed pawn to the queening square. I will present just one, without commentary. Black accurately promotes his pawn with the king's help:

13. R. Fischer – T. Petrosian

Candidates (2), Bled 1959

40...♔a7 41.♕e3 ♖d3 42.♕f4 ♕d7 43.♕c4 b6 44.♖d1 a5 45.♕f4 ♖d4 46.♕h6 b5 47.♕e3 ♔b6 48.♕h6+ ♘e6 49.♕e3 ♔a6 50.♗e2 a4 51.♕c3 ♔b6 52.♕e3 ♘c5 53.♗f3 b4 54.♕h6+ ♘e6 55.♕h8 ♕d8 56.♕h7 ♕d7 57.♕h8 b3! 58.♕b8+ ♔a5 59.♕a8+ ♔b5 60.♕b8+ ♔c4! 61.♕g8 ♔c3 62.♗h5 ♘d8 63. ♗f3 a3 64.♕f8 ♔b2 65.♕h8 ♘e6 66.♕a8 a2 67.♕a5 ♕a4 68.♖xd2+ ♔a3

0-1

Chapter 3

//

The King Finds Safe Haven

Let's explain this unusual method in simple words. When the king is in danger, normally the pieces come to its aid. In this chapter, however, we look at cases where His Majesty sets out in search of a safe place to retreat to. In this most interesting form of defense, the great Wilhelm Steinitz offers this priceless advice: "The king must defend himself!" This sounds strange, but it might not have been fully understood (at least, not by your author). Because, more often, it's the pieces that come to the king's aid; but what the great Steinitz recommended is the exception rather than the rule – although sometimes it is the only way to save a given position. We don't wish to place these two defensive methods in opposition to one another; we merely point out the exceptional nature of this latter type of defense as original and worthy of study. In a difficult position, a player might find it necessary to apply either the first method (when the pieces approach their sovereign to defend him) or the second. We must not look down on either one.

At the risk of rehashing Steinitz's idea, let me add just this one thought: in exceptional circumstances, the king can, in fact, defend himself!

I repeat: In a normal situation, the defenders can help themselves.

And now let's enjoy the play of history's first world chess champion:

1. W. Steinitz – D. Thompson
Philadelphia 1883

(see diagram next page)

19.c5!?

Steinitz plays actively, not fearing complications. Here Black should play 19...♕d8!, intending after 20.cxd6 to force a draw with 20...♖xf3+ 21.♔xf3 ♕f6+ 22.♔g3 ♕h4+ 23.♔f3 ♕f6+ (not 23...♖f8+, which lets White escape with 24.♔e2 ♕f2+ 25.♔d3) 24.♔g3 ♕h4+. Dangerous is 21.♕xf3 ♖f8, when Black would have the better chances; while 21.gxf3 just loses to 21...♕h4+.

19...♕b5?

The temptation to attack proves too strong. Now Steinitz's king will walk to the totally safe square g3. In other words, the king solves its own problems! White's bishops control all of the dangerous invasion squares.

20.cxd6 ♖e2+ 21.♔g3 ♕f5 22.♖f1

22.h4 is another way to win.

22...♘f4 23.d7+

This is enough to score the full point. But still, the cool-headed 23.♕d1!! would have given a worthy finishing touch to White's brilliant diagonal defense! Incidentally, we are dealing here with the same thing we were discussing at the beginning of the chapter: that the pieces are usually the ones that come to the aid of their king.

23...♔d8 24.♗xf4??

A shame! Steinitz passes up an excellent chance to finish the game off – in Steinitz style! – with 24.♗e2! ♘xe2 25.♔h4!!:

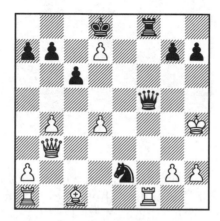

...and the king, once again, solves its own problems – brilliantly. A picturesque position!

24...♕xf4+ 25.♔h3 ♕h6+ 26.♔g3 ♕f4+ ½-½

Here Black decides to force the draw by perpetual check, although 26...g5 would have led to a win.

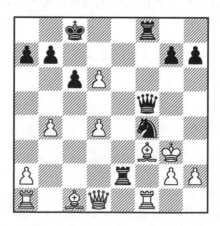

Let's go back to 23.♕d1!! (to *Fritz* 12's credit, it suggested a "Steinitz move"!):

After this, the following line is one possibility: 23...♖c2 24.♕xc2 ♕xc2 25.♗g4+ ♔d8 26.♗xf4, and the win can't be too far away.

Commenting on moves such as this, Boris Anatolievich Zlotnik, my chess teacher, would recall the words of GM and former USSR Champion Boris Gulko: Gulko would say that he experienced qualitative growth as a chessplayer when he started to understand, and then to make, backward moves.

Take note of that!

2. D. Bronstein – M. Euwe

Candidates (6), Zürich 1953

Here we have two of the strongest grandmasters of the previous century – Max Euwe, the fifth world champion; and GM David Bronstein, the planet's No. 2 chessplayer at the dawn of the '50s, who had fought then-world champion Mikhail Botvinnik to a 12:12 draw.

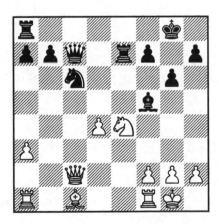

White decides to sac a knight and there followed:

20.♘f6+ ♔g7 21.♕d2

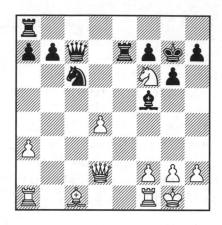

21...♔xf6!

A brave choice – and completely justified.

22.d5 ♖d8 23.♗b2+ ♘e5 24.f4 ♕c5+ 25.♔h1

25.♗d4 is an interesting alternative, e.g. 25...♖xd5 26.fxe5+ ♔e6 27.♗xc5 ♖xd2 28.♗xe7 ♔xe7 with advantage, but a probable draw.

25...♖xd5

Here 25...♔g7!? is worth looking into. The computer gives 26.fxe5 ♖xd5 27.♕g5 ♖e6 28.♖xf5? ♕c2, and the worst is over for Black. Moreover, Black now has good chances to fight for the win.

26.fxe5+

If 26.♗xe5+, then the exchange sacrifice is best: 26...♖exe5 27.fxe5+ ♔g7 28.♕b2 ♕b5, with realistic chances of getting the draw; whereas 26...♔e6 27.♕e1 ♔d7 grants his opponent a dangerous initiative. (On move 27, there is a second chance to make the same sacrifice with 27...♖xe5.)

26...♔e6

The black king seeks, and finds, his own refuge. Black apparently was afraid to play 26...♔g7 – although this appears to have been excessively cautious. On 27.♕g5, he could put the rook on e6; and if 28.♖xf5, then 28...♕c2! takes over the initiative. For example, 29.♖f6 ♖d1+ 30.♖f1 ♖xf1+ 31.♖xf1 ♕xb2 32.♕f4; and now, both 32...f6 and 32...f5 offer Black a good game.

27.♕g5 ♔d7 28.♖ac1 ♕b6 29.♗c3 ♖e8 30.♗b4

30.♕h4 promises White greater chances of fighting for the initiative.

30...♖exe5 31.♕h4

31.♕h6 is a little better.

31...a5 32.♗e1

32.♗c3 ♖e7 33.♕xh7 ♗e4! 34.♕h4 f5, when after 35.a4 White maintains his initiative, but Black's position is wholly satisfactory.

32...h5

Black has seized the initiative.

33.♗f2 ♕a6

33...♕d8, keeping up the tempo, is worth considering. Now, with the help of tactics, White manages to equalize chances.

34.♗g3 ♖e4 35.♖xf5!

A great resource. After 35.♕g5 ♖c4, Black has the upper hand.

35...♖xh4 36.♖xd5+ ♔e6 37.♖cd1 ♕c4

It's simpler to take on h4 here, followed by taking on a5, equalizing.

38.♖d6+ ♔e7 39.♖d7+ ♔f6 40.♗xh4+ ♕xh4 41.♖f1+ ♔g5

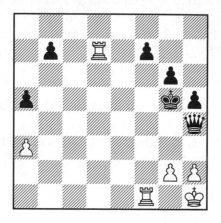

½-½

After 42.♖d5+ f5 43.♖xa5, Black's position is preferable; but it would be most difficult to exploit this.

3. R. Fischer – T. Petrosian

Candidates (16), Bled 1959

Bobby Fischer, the eleventh world champion, colorfully describes the situation in his game against Tigran Petrosian, the ninth world titleholder, in his book *My 60 Memorable Games*. Fischer exclaimed, "Got him!", referring to Black's king. There seems to be no escape for him, as the threat is 41.♕a3+ ♚b6 42.c5+, when Black must resign. Not undeservedly, however, did Petrosian have a reputation as a brilliant defender! Practice showed how tremendous his king-handling skills were; you will be persuaded of that by what follows.

40...♚b4!! 41.♕h2 ♚b3!!

"He got away again!", writes Fischer. A vivid, purely Steinitzian defensive technique, where the king itself handles its own problems, finding a place of safety right next to its knight, the latter piece controlling all of the vital squares next to the king. This maneuver would have done Steinitz proud!

42.♕a1

As before, Black's position is not devoid of danger, as shown by the following variations provided by Fischer: 42.c5 ♕xc5 (losing is 42...♕g6? 43.♗e2! ♕gg5 44.♗d1+!) 43.♕g8+ ♚a3 44.♕c2 ♕b4 45.♕a8+ ♕a4 (45...♘a4? 46.♕c1+ ♚a2 47.♕g8+ ♕b3 48.♕c2+ and wins) 46.♕cxa4+ ♘xa4 47.♕c6, with advantage for White. Grandmaster V. Ragozin believes the position would be equal if Black played 47...♘c3!; but Fischer, continuing the analysis, gives 48.♕h6!?, correctly rating this position as better for White.

Black could reach equality more simply than with Ragozin's 47...♞c3 by continuing 47...♛g5. But, instead of 44.♛c2, 44.g5! was worth considering. Also, one move later, the move 45.g5 again deserves consideration (instead of the move Fischer looked at, 45.♛a8+). To sum up: we may conclude that White had a path to victory by combining two plans –attacking the king and advancing the g-pawn at the proper moment.

Apparently, from a strategic viewpoint, White should still have played 42.c5, with which he might have set Black more serious problems; whereas now Petrosian manages to equalize through extremely accurate defense.

42...♛a3 43.♛xa3+ ♚xa3 44.♛h6

"With the idea of g4-g5-g6-g7-g8♛" – Fischer.

44...♛f7!

A very strong move.

45.♚g2

If 45.♛xc6, 45...♛f4! would be an excellent rejoinder – this is stronger than Fischer's recommendation, 45...♞d1.

45...♚b3

Intending 46...♞d1. The immediate 45...♞d1 is bad because of 46.♛c1+ ♞b2, with a good position for White.

46.♛d2 ♛h7!

Setting a trap, which Fischer falls into.

47.♚g3

47.g5 is met by 47...♕h4, when White cannot improve his position. And after 47.♗e2 ♘xe2 48.♕xe2 ♕h4, Black is better despite his material deficit.

47...♕xe4! 48.♕f2?

Fischer's question mark, although it is not quite clear yet just how he should continue. 48.dxe4? is bad: 48...♘xe4+ 49.♔h4 ♘xd2 50.g5 ♘xf1 51.g6 d3 and Black wins. And all the other lines that Fischer shows yield the same result: 48.♕xc3+? dxc3 49.dxe4 c2.

48.g5! was the move Fischer recommended, but it doesn't change things: Black has the upper hand. But there is one exception: 48.♕d1+? (Fischer's mark) 48...♘xd1 49.dxe4 ♘e3 50.♗e2 ♘xc4 51.g5 ♘d6 52.g6 ♘e8 – and here Fischer stops, considering White's position hopeless. But *Fritz* 12 suggests 53.♗d1+! and, after the bishop goes to a4, White is saved!

48...♕h1!

Here Petrosian, no doubt exhausted by the difficult defense he has conducted, accepted the proffered draw. Fischer indicated the following variation, which would support the correctness of his evaluation: 48...♕h1! 49.g5 (49.♗g2 ♕h6) 49...e4!.

½-½

We used Fischer's analysis in the above commentary.

4. M. Tal – D. Bronstein

USSR Chp, Kiev 1964

Moscow 1979: the gala event at the Polytechnic Museum, dedicated to Tigran Petrosian's 50th birthday.

To the question of which contemporary the guest of honor considered a genius chessplayer, Petrosian answered that a true genius would be a person who was ahead of his time. Then the former world champion added that, in his opinion, those people were Tal and Bronstein. Those in attendance that evening seconded Petrosian's words with tremendous applause. In this way, he gave kudos to two of the most original chessplayers on the planet, whose creations included countless novel ideas and combinations.

Now let's watch how perhaps the most mysterious players of the last century approached the following position:

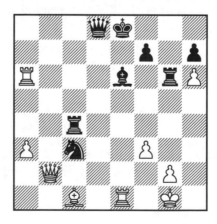

The lead-up to this situation saw Tal, from an inferior position, sacrificing a knight for counterplay. Note that, in some positions, opposite-colored bishops might serve as an argument for counterplay, whether in an attack or in the endgame. *Fritz* 12 coolly offers 32...♖c8 here, covering the eighth rank, and rates Black's position as winning (-1.70). But human thinking works very differently. Look at the game move:

32...♔e7!?

Bronstein makes an unexpected choice, playing his king to f6 – right into the pin! It certainly looks paradoxical! And in fact, after this move, *Fritz* 12's evaluation drops to (-0.90). The game continued:

33.♖a7+ ♔f6!?

The engine offers the quite sensible retreat to the eighth rank: 33...♔f8. I suggest that a human *plays chess*, whereas a chess engine *chooses between candidate moves* – a theme that we will return to in the next chapter. But, for now, we would like to anticipate the possible question from the inquisitive reader: where is the teachable moment in this king maneuver? For, to the untrained eye, it's perfectly obvious that *Fritz* offers to play a stronger move than GM Bronstein, although the evaluation of the position following the king maneuver isn't so bad (-0.54 according to *Fritz*). Let's take a stab at answering this question.

In the first place, this is not a "test" position, where the king's flight from the dangerous rank can be seen as best. With other strategic techniques, there are cases where it (that is, the technique) could be the most direct and the strongest, and in other circumstances it could be an alternative to the best continuation. Your author's task is to select the technique; this where the value of the present work lies. And secondly, we repeat that sometimes the player tries an unusual move with the goal of setting his opponent a problem which he must solve over the board; and that sometimes gives the opponent a hard time.

Now see how one of the most dangerous chessplayers of all time makes a mistake – but it doesn't make him lose! The most engrossing part of the game is still to come!

34.♖e4

Loses. He had to play 34.♗e3. Here Bronstein examines the following variations: 34...♕d3 35.♕b8 ♘d5 (35...♖c8 36.♕f4+; 35...♘e2+ 36.♖xe2) 36.♕h8+ ♔f5.

Now look at the diagram below:

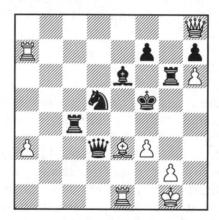

A beautiful position! White can't play 37.g4+ on account of 37...♖cxg4+ 38.fxg4 ♖xg4+ 39.♔f2 ♕c2+ 40.♖e2 ♖g2+! and wins. If he tries to maintain the tension with 37.♖a5, then 37...♕c2! is strong: 38.♗f2 ♕c3 forces the queen trade. The careless 37...♕c3 would lead, after 38.♕xc3 ♖xc3 39.g4+ ♔e5 40.♗d2+, to an ending where both sides have approximately equal chances.

This is all correct, and quite interesting. But unfortunately, with 36.♕d8+ White would break up Black's plan: on 36...♔f5, the move 37.♖a5 becomes still stronger.

We'll also add that Black could avoid all of these head-spinning variations simply by playing 34...♕d5 (instead of 34...♕d3).

For those who suffer from insomnia and want to get at the truth, we recommend analyzing this position.

The actual game continued:

34...♕d1+ 35.♔h2 ♖xe4 36.♕xc3+

36.fxe4 meets with 36...♕h5+ 37.♔g1 ♕c5+ (Bronstein).

36...♖e5!

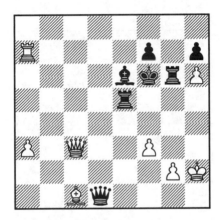

Unbelievable! It sure looks crazy, doesn't it? Now the rook is pinned; but here, too, Black successfully untangles himself. Bronstein offers this variation leading to a draw: 36...♕d4 37.♕xd4+ ♖xd4 38.♗b2 ♖xh6+ 39.♔g1 ♖h4 40.♖a4 ♔e5, and now 41.g4 – but not 41.g3, as the grandmaster gives, because Black then wins with 41...♔d5.

37.♗f4

Here, if White plays 37.♖a5, Black wins with either 37...♕e2! or 37...♕e1.

37...♕e2 38.♗xe5+ ♕xe5+ 39.♕xe5+ ♔xe5 40.♖a5+ ♔d4 41.♖h5 ♗d5 42.♔h3 f5 0-1

White resigned here. Bronstein gives a variation where the king – the hero of our book – could put the finishing touches on this truly "royal" game: 43.♔h2 ♔e3 44.♖xf5 ♔f2.

This game fragment was full of the most interesting pins and unpins!

5. M. Tal – T. Petrosian

USSR Chp, Yerevan 1975

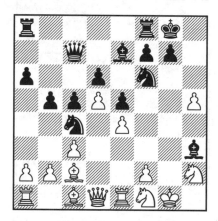

White has a simple plan: ♕f3, b2-b3, and ♘e3 or ♘g3; and then, at the right time, jumping to f5 with a possible attack on the king. Petrosian decided that there was no point in waiting and the time had come for decisive action, where the king would seek safety in its own camp. Thus there followed:

17...g6!

Whereas the computer – to general astonishment – suggests the waiting and planless tactic 17...♔h8, followed by 18.♕f3 ♗d7, rating Black's position highly, which it is difficult to agree with. We won't be surprised if it changes its assessment after a few moves. After the game move, in our opinion Black breathes more easily. The king becomes a mobile piece; the f5 square is taken under control; and the rook gets the h-file.

18.♘g3 ♔g7 19.♔h1

A bit risky: Tal is trying to make use of the g-file, but this plan has a clear shortcoming: the uncomfortable position of the white king. *Fritz* offers 19.h6+. Tal fundamentally opposes closing up the position.

19...♖h8 20.♖g1 ♔f8

Petrosian handles the king masterfully!

21.a4 ♘b6 22.axb5 axb5 23.♖xa8+ ♘xa8 24.hxg6 fxg6 25.♘gf1 ♔f7

His Majesty dances on a very small floor!

26.♕f3 ♕c8 27.♗g5 ♗xf1

Black seeks to simplify the position as much as possible by trading off White's powerful bishop.

28.♖xf1 ♕g4

Now White definitely needs to be careful.

29.♕g2?!

29.♕g3 is necessary in order to meet 29...♕e2 with 30.♗d3, since after 30...♕xb2, White can play either 31.f4 or 31.♖g1, setting Black some problems. But in order to reach equality, Black still has to play very accurately. That's why 29...♘b6, with clear equality, is worth considering.

29...♘b6

Black passes up the opportunity to play the natural 29...♕xg2+ 30.♔xg2 ♘xd5 (see diagram below), with a pawn to the good; although in that case, White would have the a-file and the advantage of the bishop pair, which would level out the chances.

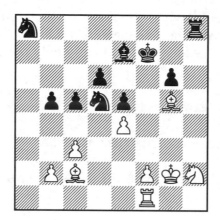

Now the draw is clear.

30.♗xf6 ♕xg2+ 31.♔xg2 ♗xf6 32.♖a1 ♖a8 33.♖xa8 ♘xa8 34.♘f3 ♘b6 35.♔f1 ½-½

6. A. Petrosian – G. Zaichik

Kirovakan 1978

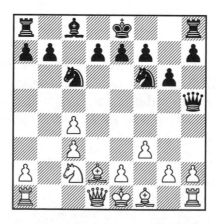

In this game, the white pieces were handled by future grandmaster Arshak Petrosian.

10.e4 ♘xe4

Courageous, though dubious. Besides, Arshak Petrosian manages his king play with great confidence. In this regard – and also in the subtlety of his positional understanding – he reminds one of his great predecessor, Tigran Petrosian. Is it possible that the last name is to "blame" for this?

11.fxe4 ♕h4+ 12.♔e2 d5 13.♘e3 d4 14.cxd4 ♘xd4+ 15.♔d3 ♘e6 16.♘d5 ♘c5+ 17.♔c2

Let's consider 17.♔d4 – in the spirit of our book – and if 17... ♘xe4, then 18.♕e1! could stop Black's attack cold:

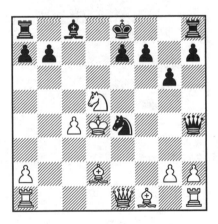

But let's go back to our game.

17...♕xe4+ 18.♔b2 ♗f5 19.♖c1

Here White need not have feared executing the kind of fork so beloved by beginners – that is, 19.♘c7+. But there's another detail, so highly valued by Armenia's former world champion: safety and security above all!

19...0-0-0 20.♕e1

Once again, played safely, taking the queen away from possible confrontation with the enemy rook, just in case. Whereas the courageous 20.♗c3 would have set more problems for Black.

20...♕d4+ 21.♗c3 ♘a4+ 22.♔b3

Arshak Petrosian feels so secure about his king play that he doesn't even take this opportunity to tuck His Majesty safely away in the corner with 22.♔a1.

But now, the king's fantastic voyage concludes safely:

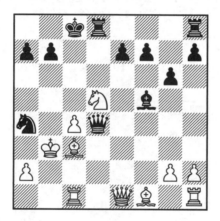

22...♘xc3 23.♕xc3

23.♘xe7+ is also quite playable here.

White went on to make successful use of his material advantage. Yes, there were times when both sides might have played more strongly, including at one point when Black might have had serious drawing chances.

23...♕c5 24.♗d3 ♗xd3 25.♕xd3 e6 26.♕e3! ♕xe3+ 27. ♘xe3 ♖d2 28.♖c2 ♖hd8 29.♖hc1 29...♖8d3+ 30.♔b2 ♖xc2+ 31.♘xc2 ♖d2 32.♖g1 ♔c7 33.h4 ♖f2 34.g3 f5 35.♖e1 ♔d6 36.♖d1+ ♔e7 37.♖d3 ♖g2 38.♔c3 e5 39.a3 e4 40.♖e3 ♔f6 41.♘b4 a5 42.♘d5+ ♔e5 43.♘f4 ♖a2 44.♘d3+ ♔f6 45.♔b3

♖d2 46.♘f4 h6 47.♔c3 ♖a2 48.♔d4 ♖d2+ 49.♔c3 ♖a2
50.♔d4 ♖d2+ 51.♔c5 g5 52.♘d5+ ♔e5 53.♖b3 f4 54.gxf4+
gxf4 55.♖xb7 f3 56.♖e7+ ♔f5 57.♘c3 1-0

This game reminds me a lot of the variation in the Slav Defense
with a piece sacrifice on e4: 1.d4 d5 2.c4 c6 3.♘f3 ♘f6 4.♘c3 dxc4
5.a4 ♗f5 6.♘e5 e6 7.f3 ♗b4 8.e4 ♗xe4 9.fxe4 ♘xe4 10.♗d2 ♕xd4
11.♘xe4 ♕xe4+ 12.♕e2 ♗xd2+ 13.♔xd2 ♕d5+ 14.♔c2, where there
are quite a lot of games featuring our theme.

7. G. Agzamov – L. Psakhis

Frunze 1979

Black's advantage is based on his more aggressively placed
pieces and having a clear plan of action. His only problem is the
king's somewhat shaky position. Here, 32...♕f7! would set White
big problems. Actually, the move he played is also good.

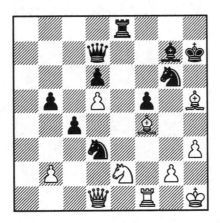

32...♖e4 33.♗xg6+?

In hopes of mounting a dubious attack on the king. Probably
a bit better is 33.♗c1, although 33...♘ge5 would give Black a very
pleasant position.

33...♔xg6 34.♘g3

It's too late for 34.♗c1 on account of 34...♕e7; it looks like 34.♗d2 had to be played. But now Black bravely snaps off the bishop. White really doesn't have enough men for the attack, so Black easily parries the threats.

34...♖xf4 35.♕h5+ ♔f6 36.♖xf4 ♘xf4 37.♕h4+ ♔e5 38.♘f1 ♗f6 39.♕g3 ♕a7! 40.♘d2 ♕a1+ 41.♔h2 ♔xd5 0-1

8. M. Chiburdanidze – L. Psakhis

Riga 1980
Sicilian Defense B97

1.e4 c5 2.♘f3 d6 3.d4 cxd4 4.♘xd4 ♘f6 5.♘c3 a6 6.♗g5 e6 7.f4 ♕b6 8.♕d2 ♕xb2 9.♖b1 ♕a3 10.f5 ♘c6 11.fxe6 fxe6 12.♘xc6 bxc6 13.e5 dxe5 14.♗f6 gxf6 15.♘e4 ♗e7 16.♗e2 h5 17.♖b3 ♕a4

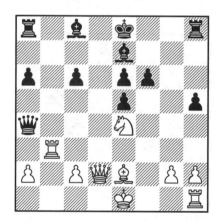

18.♘xf6+

A well-known position, very popular in the '60s. Bobby Fischer, for one, liked defending it for Black. And he did it very well indeed. Whoever wants to really study the history of this variation would find it simplest to study the games of the legendary eleventh world champion. Even in his 1972 World Championship match with

Boris Spassky, he resorted to his favorite variation twice. Note that, after the knight sacrifice, Black has to demonstrate a great mastery of king play. Note, too, that *Fritz* 12 rates the position as -0.56, and gives thumbs down to the knight sacrifice, suggesting 18.c4 instead. We think that such variations may have lost – or are losing – their topicality, with the onset of new and powerful computer chess engines.

18...♗xf6 19.c4 ♗e7

Fritz suggests making this retreat after a preliminary check on h4, taking the g3 square away from White's rook.

20.0-0 ♖a7

And here it suggests 20...h4.

21.♖b8 ♖c7 22.♗d3

Moving the queen to d3 would have been better, with very dangerous threats.

22...♖g8 23.♕e2 ♕a3 24.♔h1

Now it's the black king's turn.

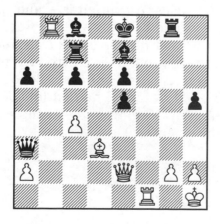

24...♔d8! 25.c5 ♖f8 26.♖fb1 ♗xc5 27.♗xa6 ♗d4! 28.♗c4 ♔e7! 29.♕xh5 ♕c3 30.♕h7+ ♔d6! 31.♕h6 ♖ff7 32.♗e2 ♕e3 33.♕h5 ♖h7 34.♕f3 ♕xf3 35.♗xf3 ♖b7 0-1

9. V. Korchnoi – A. Yusupov

Lone Pine 1981

With his previous move, 32...♖b8-a8, Black – apparently tired of defending passively – decided to make use of the first rank for counterplay. It would seem natural here to play 33.♖xb5, after which there might follow 33...♖a1 34.♗xc4 ♖xe1+ 35.♗f1, with drawish tendencies. A computer – and, probably, a lot of grandmasters – would have played this way, but not Viktor Korchnoi, a man who always strove for an uncompromising fight and the chance to avoid the well-trodden path, preferring his own, original way. An excellent example to emulate! In the period 1974-1981, GM Korchnoi battled for the title of World Champion with Anatoly Karpov, and was the second strongest chessplayer on the planet.

The game continued:

33.♔f1!! ♖a1 34.♔e2!!

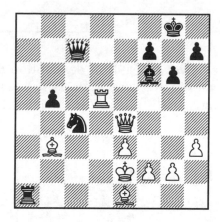

Just two moves have been played since our first diagram – and yet, how things have changed in the interim! Apparently unable to adjust to the new situation, Artur Yusupov went on to lose within a few moves. We note, for the sake of objectivity, that the position was not easy to play for Black, whereas the white pieces stand ready to strike, interacting beautifully with each other. The king stands triumphant!

34...♔g7

Here 34...♕c8!? is worth considering, perhaps continuing 35.♗b4 ♕a8 36.♗xc4 bxc4 37.♕xc4, when although White has a clear advantage, Black retains saving chances.

35.♗b4! ♘b6 36.♖d6!?

Once again, played like a human. There were terrible threats hanging over Black. The computer's choice, 36.♖xb5, would also have maintained a great advantage.

36...♖c1

Now comes a tactical blow that flows out of the position itself.

37.♖xf6! ♔xf6 38.♕d4+ ♔g5 39.♗e7+ ♕xe7 1-0

Black resigned without waiting for White's reply.

10. G. Kasparov – T. Petrosian

Tilburg 1981

Garry Kasparov gives a beautiful description of this game in his book, *The Test of Time* (Pergamon, 1986). (The game is also extensively annotated in the *ChessBase* database.)

30.a4

Threatening to establish a bind with 31.♖cb2 and 32.♕b1; therefore, Black's reply is more or less forced.

30...b5

Next came:

31.axb5 cxb5 32.♖a2! ♔b7!!?

This was the first surprise for Kasparov. Kasparov was amazed that Petrosian made this move so quickly, while avoiding such traps as 32...bxc4 33.♖xa6+!; and 32...♗d6 33.♖xb5 ♖xb5 34.♘xd6 ♕xd6 35.♕xb5.

33.♗b4?

The alternative 33.♘a3! will be treated in greater detail following the end of the game.

33...♕e8!

And here Black successfully avoided these traps: 33...♕d8? 34.e4! fxe4 35.♕xe4 ♕e8 (35...bxc4 36.♕xe6 ♘7b6 37.♖b1) 36.♕xd5+ exd5 37.♗xd5+ ♔a7 38.♖xa6+ ♔xa6 39.♖a3+ ♗a5 40.♖xa5#.

34.♗d6

In the line 34.♗a5 ♕e7! 35.♗e1 ♗b6 36.♘xb6 ♔xb6 37.♕d2 ♖c6 38.♕a5+ ♔b7 39.♗b4 ♕d8 40.♕a3 ♖a8, White keeps his advantage, but Black still holds.

34...♖a8 35.♕b1

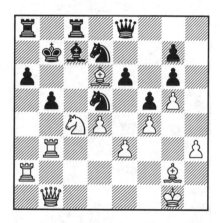

Here, Kasparov writes that he had set up his pieces for the strike, expecting to deliver the decisive blow at the proper moment. But unexpectedly, there came:

35...♔c6!!

– and this sharp turnaround knocked him completely off balance. Petrosian made this king move, as Kasparov wrote, instantaneously – with amazing ease! White was in shock (as well as in time pressure), and lost quickly as a result.

36.♖ba3?

36.♗xc7 bxc4 (if 36...♔xc7, then 37.♘b2 ♔d8 38.♕e1) 37.♖b7
♖xc7 38.♖xa6+ ♖xa6 39.♕b5+ ♔d6 40.♕xa6+ ♔e7 (40...♖c6?
41.♕a3+) 41.♗xd5 ♖xb7 42.♗xb7 (42.♕xe6+? ♔d8 43.♕xe8+ ♔xe8
44.♗xb7 c3, and Black wins) 42...♕b8 43.♔f2 would have given him
a small advantage.

**36...bxc4 37.♖xa6+ ♖xa6 38.♖xa6+ ♗b6 39.♗c5 ♕d8
40.♕a1**

If 40.♕b4, then 40...♖a8 41.♕a4+ ♔b7.

40...♘xc5 41.dxc5 ♔xc5 42.♖a4 0-1

Now let's return to the position after move 32, with the comments and variations offered by Kasparov.

Together, we will follow the course of this remarkable grandmaster's thinking. Here's how he explains the basics of this position,
and the keys we must use to unlock it.

Black's position is held together by the knight on d5. If it is driven
away from there, the entire position will collapse like a house of
cards. So we have to 1) attack the strongest piece (in this case, that
knight on d5); and 2) undermine its support (in this case, the pawn
on e6). Now you will better understand the white knight's maneuver
(♘a3-c2-b4) and the pawn breaks 36.e4 and 40.d5.

Watch how White could have consistently carried out the general plan:

33.♘a3! ♗b6

If 33...♘7b6, then 34.♘xb5 axb5 35.♕xb5 ♖d8 (35...♖a8 36.♗xd5+ exd5 37.♕xd5+) 36.♗b4! ♕e8 37.♕a6+ ♔c6 38.♗c5 ♔d7 (38...♖a8 39.♖xb6+) 39.♗f1!, with a winning position.

34.♘c2! ♖a8 35.♘b4 ♕d6 36.e4

A well thought-out move, but it meets with a concrete refutation. 36.♖bb2! would have been more cautious, getting the rook away from possible attacks and keeping a dangerous initiative.

36...fxe4 37.♕xe4 ♖a7 38.♕xg6 ♗xd4+ 39.♔h1 ♘7b6 40.f5!, and White has gotten to the knight's support! An instructive lesson in positional play from the thirteenth world champion. Although Kasparov himself gives the following drawing line: 36...♘c5! (instead of 36...fxe4) 37.dxc5 ♕xc5+ 38.♔h2 ♕g1+ 39.♔g3 ♕f2+, with perpetual check.

Evacuating the King
From an Impending Attack

In this part of the book, we examine games in which one player removes his king to a safer place ahead of his own or his opponent's pawn storm or piece attack. Before taking up chapters 4 and 5, we note with interest that this strategic technique is not considered at all by *Fritz* 12. Fritz totally fails to consider this kind of method.

Chapter 4

//

Evacuating the King Ahead of Your Opponent's Attack

1. W. Steinitz – D. Martínez

Philadelphia 1882

In this position, White has launched a pawn storm to pry open the g-file, so the king has to be evacuated. But this is our own, human, feeling about it. *Fritz* 12, on the other hand, rates Black's position as "winning" (!) and suggests playing 14...♕b6.

14...♔f8!? 15.h4 ♕c7 16.♕g2 ♔e7 17.♘e3 ♕d6 18.c3 ♖f8 19.♘c2 ♗b6 20.exd5?

A terrible mistake. After 20.♗e3, the game is about equal, although one might still prefer Black's position.

20...♘c5 21.♗a2 cxd5?

Returning the favor. 21...♘xd3+ wins.

22.♕e2 e4 23.dxe4 ♕g3+ 24.♔d1 ♘fxe4

24...♘cxe4 is stronger.

25.♗e3

Another possibility is 25.♘e3.

25...♖fd8 26.♖h3

And 26.♘d4 is worth looking into.

26...♕c7 27.♘d4 ♘a4?! 28.♘xb5 ♕d7 29.♗xb6 ♘xb6 30.♘d4

White has a winning position.

30...♖h8 31.♘xf7 ♔xf7 32.♕xe4 ♗a6 33.♕e6+ ♕xe6 34. fxe6+ ♔e7 35.♖g3 ♖ag8 36.♔c2 ♘c8 37.♖ag1 ♖h7 38.♗b1

Why not 38.♗xd5 ?

38...♘d6 39.♔c1 ♘e4 40.h5 ♔f8 41.♖f3+ ♔e8 42.♖f7 ♗c8 43.♖f5 ♗b7 44.♗d3 ♖f8 45.♖xf8+ ♔xf8 46.♖f1+ ♔e8 47.♖f7 ♗a6 48.♗xe4

And here, the simplest move is 48.♗xa6.

48...dxe4 49.♘c6 ♖h6 50.♖e7+ ♔f8 51.b4

51.♖a7 is simpler.

51...axb4 52.axb4 g5 53.b5

Now 53.♖a7 is better.

53...g4

Preferable is 53...♗xb5 – although, after 54.♖f7+ ♔e8 55.♘d4, White would still have a winning position.

54.b6

Why not take the bishop?

54...♖xh5 55.b7 ♖b5 56.♖f7+ ♔g8 57.b8♕+ ♖xb8 58.♘xb8 1-0

2. L. van Fleet – A. Nimzowitsch

Ostend 1907

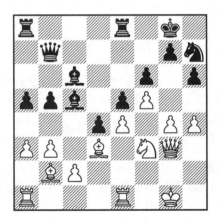

A typical situation, with a qualitative pawn majority (at least, according to Nimzowitsch) for White. Everything hinges on the g4-g5 pawn break. Both sides must make the necessary preparations for the opening of the position. White's game looks preferable to us; but here it's important to choose the right moment to carry out the breakthrough.

Nimzowitsch was one of the strongest players of the last century, the author of two famous books on positional play, *My System* and *Chess Praxis*. In fact, Nimzowitsch was one of those who continued the teachings of the great Steinitz. His book was bedside reading for many players; and for Tigran Petrosian, as Tigran Vartanovich himself said (in jest, of course), it was "the book I kept under my pillow."

26...♔f7 27.♖e2

27.g5 immediately might be better.

27...♖h8!

The well-known "mysterious rook move" – played by the man who invented it!

28.♔g2 ♘f8 29.g5 hxg5 30.hxg5 ♘d7

The knight takes up a very useful defensive position, and a comfortable path opens up for the king's evacuation: f7-e7-d6-c7.

31.gxf6?!

Dubious: within a couple of moves it will be Black who controls the g-file.

31...gxf6 32.♘h4

The following variation would be typical: 32.♕g6+ ♔e7 33.♖h1 ♖xh1 34.♔xh1 ♖h8+ 35.♔g1 ♕a8!, gaining control of the open lines and then invading White's camp.

32...♖ag8 33.♘g6 ♖h5 34.♔f2 ♘f8 35.♖g1 ♖g5 36.♕h4 ♖xg1

36...♘xg6 at once is stronger.

37.♔xg1 ♘xg6 38.♕h5! ♔f8 39.fxg6 ♕g7 40.♖g2 ♖h8 41.♕e2 ♖h4 42.♗c1

Now for the finale:

42...♖xe4! 43.♕d2 ♖h4 44.♕xa5 ♕d7 45.g7+ ♔g8 46.♗c4+ bxc4 47.♕xc5 ♖h1+ 0-1

3. A. Alekhine – A. Nimzowitsch

St. Petersburg 1914

White has a dangerous attack. Standing at the edge of the cliff, Black shows great resourcefulness in defense, succeeding in his main task: to get his king away from the danger zone.

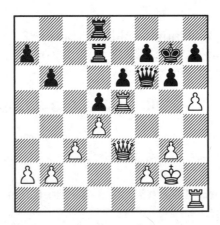

29...♔f8 30.♖h4 ♔e8 31.♕h6 ♔e7 32.♖f4 ♕h8 33.♖e1 ♖c8 34.♖h1 ♕g8 35.♕g5+ ♔d6 36.♕e5+ ♔c6 37.a4

All the commentators censured this move; and in fact, later on it was precisely due to this weakness that White fell into a difficult position. But, to be objective, we should point out that this was not the losing move. After the move, White's position is still good.

37...♔b7

That's it – the king is out of danger. Later, in the war of maneuver, Black even manages to win. As they say, we are rewarded for our persistence and creativity.

38.♖a1 ♕e8

Also possible is 38...a6, so as to reply to 39.a5 with 39...b5.

39.♖f6 ♕d8 40.♖f3 ♕h8 41.♕e2 a6 42.♕e3 ♕g7 43.h6

Nor did the commentators like this move, although it is hard to suggest anything better.

43...♕f8 44.♕e5 ♕h8 45.♖f6 ♕f8 46.♖h1 ♕d8 47.♖f4 ♖c4 48.♖a1 ♖c6 49.♖f6 ♕b8 50.♕e3 ♖e7 51.♕f3 ♕e8 52.g4 ♕d7 53.♖e1 ♖c7 54.b3 ♔a7 55.g5 ♕d6 56.♕d3 ♕a3 57.♕c2 ♕b4 58.♖c1 ♕d6 59.♕d3 ♕a3 60.♖b1

White was wrong to turn down the repetition: the queen invasion plays right into Black's hands.

60...♕a2 61.♖f3

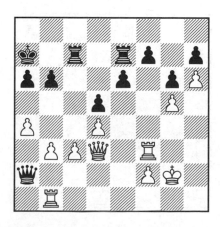

61...e5!

The long-awaited breakthrough! Now the initiative passes permanently over to Black.

62.♖e3 e4 63.♕d1 f5 64.gxf6 ♖f7 65.♖a1 ♕b2 66.♖b1

66.♕b1 would have given White some chances. Evidently, the sudden turn of events had its effect on Alekhine. Truth be told, it's hard to play positions like this one. Black's pieces finish each other's sentences, so to speak – working more harmoniously together. The same cannot be said for his opponent's pieces. Here too, it would be useful to mention that, as a rule, difficult positions give rise to further mistakes.

66...♕a3 67.c4

67.f3 is worth considering.

67...♖xf6 68.cxd5 ♖cf7 69.♖e2 ♕d6 70.♕c2 ♕xd5 71.♔f1 e3 72.♖xe3 ♕h1+ 73.♔e2 ♖xf2+ 74.♔d3 ♕d5 75.♕c8 ♖d7 0-1

4. A. Becker – A. Nimzowitsch

Breslau 1925

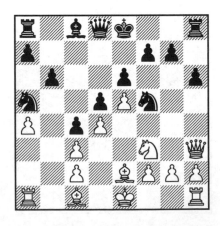

White stands a little better, with a clear plan. In order to avoid falling into a lost position, it is important for Black to determine where to put his king. Facing the threat of the pawn storm g2-g4 and f2-f4-f5, and also considering the closed nature of the position in the center and on the queenside, it would be sensible to think about castling long. But could he not instead save a tempo with 13...♔d7, as played in the game? In that case, Black would keep the choice to arrange his queenside pieces more logically. Note, too, that this way he also solves the problem of connecting his rooks. Looking ahead, we note that there are many examples of this kind in the French Defense and other openings featuring a closed pawn center. So now White considers himself obligated to open the game with pawn breaks.

13...♔d7 14.g4 ♘e7 15.♘d2 ♕e8 16.f4 ♔c7 17.♗a3 ♗d7 18.♕f3 h5!

Striving, little by little, to wrest the initiative from White.

19.♘xc4!?

A brave choice. White could also play the quiet 19.h3.

19...♘xc4 20.♗xc4 hxg4 21.♕g2 ♘f5

21...f5!? 22.♗d6+ ♔b7 is also worth considering.

22.♗d3 ♗xa4! 23.♗xf5 exf5 24.♕xd5

Black is for preference after 24.c4 ♕c6 25.♕xd5 ♕xd5 26.cxd5 ♗b5!.

24...♗c6 25.♕d6+ ♔c8 26.d5 ♖h6 27.e6 ♗xd5

Black failed to pull the trigger with 27...♖xe6+! 28.dxe6 ♗xh1 29.0-0-0 ♗f3 30.exf7 ♕xf7 31.♕d8+ ♔b7 32.♖d7+ ♔a6, when he would have had the better chances. *Fritz* doesn't miss such opportunities. It also examines the "computer move" 27...♗xa4, which it views as best.

28.♕xd5 ♕xe6+ 29.♕xe6+ ♖xe6+ 30.♔d2 ♔b7

The journey is complete. Chances are about even. The game now proceeds toward what should have been a draw.

31.♖ae1 ♖h8 32.♖xe6 fxe6 33.♖e1 ♖xh2+ 34.♔d3 g3 35.♖g1 ♖h3 36.♔d4 ♔c6 37.♖g2 a5 38.c4 ♖h2 39.♖xg3 ♖xc2 40.♖xg7 ♖e2 41.♗c1 ♖e4+ 42.♔d3 b5 43.cxb5+ ♔xb5 44.♗e3 ♔c6 45.♖f7 a4 46.♖f8 a3 47.♖a8 e5 48.♖a6+ ♔b5 49.♖b6+ ♔a5

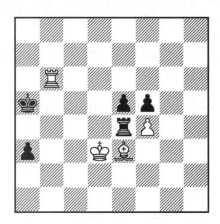

50.♖f6

This leads to needless complications. Simply 50.♖b8 leads to an easy draw.

50...a2 51.♗d2+ ♔b5 52.♗c3 ♖d4+! 53.♔e2

And this makes his defensive task much harder. 53.♔c2 would be a draw.

53...♖xf4 54.♖f8 ♔c4 55.♗a1 ♖e4+ 56.♔d2 f4

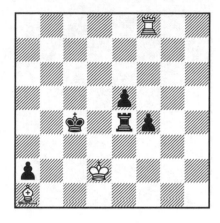

57.♖c8+?

And now this leads straight to defeat – although, for a tired player, it wouldn't be too easy to find 57.♔d1!, intending to attack the a-pawn with the rook.

57...♔d5 58.♖d8+ ♔e6 59.♖e8+ ♔f5 60.♖g8 f3 0-1

A few more game fragments on our theme:

5. P. Romanovsky – J. Vilner

Moscow 1927

Up to a certain point, Black defends very inventively.

(see diagram next page)

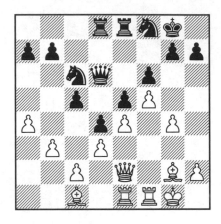

26...♔f7 27.g5 ♔e7 28.♖f3 ♔d7 29.♖g3 ♔c8 30.gxf6 gxf6 31.♗f3 ♘d7 32.♕g2 a5?!

32...♘e7 gives a decent game. Now White gains the upper hand and, with his solid control of the g-file, brings the game to victory.

33.♗h5 ♖e7 34.♖g8 ♘b6 35.♗h6 ♖c7 36.♖d1 ♘b4 37.♖d2 ♔b8 38.♕g3 ♔a7 39.♖g2 ♘c8 40.♕f2 ♘c6 41.♖2g3 ♔a6 42.♕g2 ♖cd7 43.♗e8 ♖c7 44.♗f8 ♘6e7 45.♗f7 ♕b6 46.♗xe7 ♖xe7 47.♖xd8 ♕xd8 48.♖g8 ♕c7 49.♗e6 ♘a7 50.h4 ♘c6 51.h5 ♔a7 52.h6 ♘d8 53.♗d5 ♘f7 54.♕g7 ♕b6 55.♗xf7 ♕b4 56.♕xf6 ♕e1+ 57.♔h2 ♕f2+ 58.♖g2 ♕f4+ 59.♔h3 ♕f3+ 60.♖g3 ♕h1+ 61.♔g4 ♕d1+ 62.♔h4 ♕h1+ 63.♔g5 ♕c1+ 64.♔h5 ♕h1+ 65.♕h4 ♕d1+ 66.♕g4 1-0

6. R. Byrne – A. Kotov

New York 1954

There's no doubt White has the advantage. He can undertake kingside operations. Therefore, Black seeks safety by moving his king over to the more secure queen's wing.

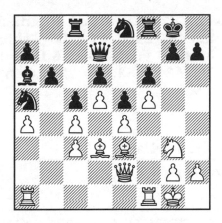

17...♔f7 18.♖f3 ♔e7 19.♘f1 ♔d8 20.♖h3 ♖h8 21.g4 ♔c7 22.♘g3 ♔b8

The evacuation is complete. Despite his advantage, White was unable to break through Black's defenses.

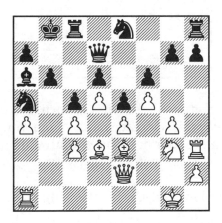

23.♔f2 ♘c7 24.♕a2 ♖cd8 25.♖g1 ♕e7 26.♗e2 ♗c8 27.♘f1 ♗d7 28.♘d2 g5 29.♘f1 ♗e8 30.♘g3 h6 31.♘h5 ♗xh5 32. gxh5 ♘e8 33.♗g4 ♘g7 34.♔e2 ♔c7 35.♔d3 ♖a8 36.♖b1 ♖hb8

37.♖b2 a6 38.♔c2 ♕d7 39.♖g3 ♕e8 40.♗d2 ♖a7 41.♖h3 b5 42.axb5 axb5 43.cxb5 ♖xb5 44.♖xb5 ♕xb5 45.c4 ♕xc4+ 46.♕xc4 ♘xc4 47.♗xg5 ♘xf5 48.exf5 fxg5 49.f6 e4 50.f7 ♖a8 51.♖c3 ♘e5 52.♖a3 ♖f8 53.♗e6 ♔b6 54.♖b3+ ♔c7 55.♖a3 ♔b6 56.♖b3+ ½-½

7. D. Yanofsky – L. Portisch

Stockholm Interzonal 1962

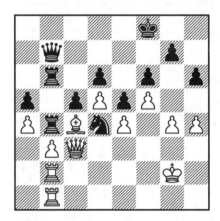

Black's position is good – but how to turn it into a win? There is no simple answer to this. Here it can't be done without some "help" from his opponent. A poor position not infrequently leads to poor moves; that's what wiser men say, anyway.

In order to pre-empt g4-g5, Black's king takes itself out of the danger zone.

39...♔e8 40.♔f2 ♔d8 41.h5

White naively bails out Black. Notice how the black king proceeds to run back to the same corner, which is now safe. The time has come for Black to begin decisive operations on the queenside.

41...♔e7 42.♔g2 ♔f8 43.♔f2 ♔f7 44.♔g2 ♔g8 45.♔f2 ♔h7

That's it – he's arrived! Now Black can try breaking through on the opposite wing.

46.♔e3 ♕a7 47.♔f2 ♖b8 48.♔g2 ♖xc4!?

Let's get the party started! Lajos Portisch's complex strategy leaves us deeply impressed. Fine king play alternates with an energetic attack and a decisive incursion! Only "iron" *Fritz* could hold this position for White; for a human, it's practically impossible.

49.♕xc4

After 49.bxc4 ♖b4, only Black has winning chances, although it's not a slam dunk.

49...♖b4 50.♕c3 ♕a6 51.♔f2 c4 52.bxc4 ♖xc4 53.♕a3 ♕c8 54.♖d2 ♖c3 55.♕b2 ♕c4 56.♔g2 ♘b3 57.♖e2 ♕d3 58.♖be1 ♘d4 59.♔h1 ♕h3+ 60.♖h2 ♕f3+ 61.♔g1 ♕g3+ 62.♔f1 ♘f3 0-1

8. J. Díez del Corral – T. Petrosian

Palma de Mallorca 1969

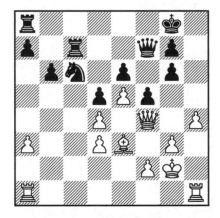

From a static perspective, Black's position looks more pleasant: good knight vs. bad bishop, plus Black has the better pawn structure. But a dynamic evaluation clearly favors White. He threatens h4-h5 with a brutal attack on the opposing king. Any opening of the position could easily lead to an immediate win for White. Once again we witness a beautiful display of how to hold a difficult position, as Petrosian demonstrates his great command of the king and leads his monarch to safety.

22...♔f8! 23.♕g5 ♔e8 24.♖ac1 ♔d7 25.h5 gxh5 26.♖xh5 ♖g8! 27.♖h7 ♔c8! 28.♕h4 ♕g6 29.♖h8 ♖xh8 30.♕xh8+ ♔b7

Success! Now watch how Petrosian outplays his opponent from here on out.

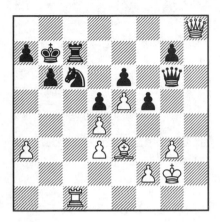

31.♕f8 ♖c8!

Next step: driving the active queen out of Black's camp.

32.♕d6 ♕e8! 33.a4 ♖d8! 34.♕a3 ♕e7! 35.♕c3 ♖c8 36. ♗d2 g5

Starting the pawn storm!

37.♕c2 f4! 38.gxf4 gxf4 39.♗xf4 ♖g8+ 40.♗g3?!

40.♔f1 is better.

40...♘xd4

Beautiful coordination between the knight and the long-range pieces! Black stays on top in the hand-to-hand combat that follows.

41.♕c3 ♘e2 42.♕c6+ ♔b8 43.♖e1 ♘f4+ 44.♔f1 ♘xd3 45.♖b1 ♕f7 46.♕d6+ ♔b7 47.♔e2 ♖c8!

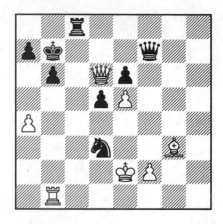

The decisive penetration.

48.a5 ♖c2+ 49.♔f1 ♘xf2 50.♖xb6+

Desperation in a lost position.

50...axb6 51.♕xb6+ ♔c8 52.♕a6+ ♔b8 53.♕b6+ ♕b7 54.♕d6+ ♕c7 0-1

9. E. Gufeld – M. Taimanov

USSR Chp, Moscow 1969

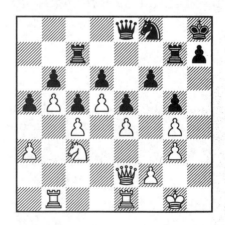

Here too, evacuating the king enables Black to hold.

1...♔g8! 2.♔g2 ♔f7 3.♖h1 ♔e7 4.♖h5 ♔d8 5.♖bh1 ♔c8 6. ♘d1 ♖cf7 7.♘e3 ♖g6 8.♘f5 ♔c7, and the game ended in a draw.

10. K. Vshivkov – A. Terekhin

USSR 1989

1...f5 doesn't look too bad in this position, but Black is attracted by the unusual idea of evacuating his king to a7.

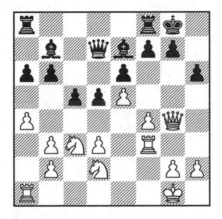

1...g6!? 2.♖h3 ♔g7 3.♘f1 ♖h8 4.♘g3 ♔f8 5.♖f1?! ♔e8 6.♘ge2 ♔d8 7.d4 ♔c7 8.♖c1 ♔b8 9.♖d3 h5 10.♕f3 ♔a7

10...c4 is worth a look. After the game move, White should prefer either 11.dxc5 or 11.a5.

11.♘a2?! ♖ac8 12.♖dc3 c4 13.bxc4? dxc4, with a great advantage for Black.

Chapter 5

Removing the King Ahead of Your Own Attack

1. V. Smyslov – V. Panov

Moscow 1943

Before undertaking a pawn attack, it is completely logical for White to transfer his king to the relative safety of the queenside.

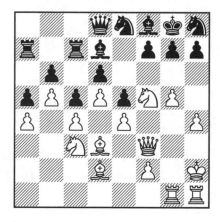

31.♔g2 g6 32.♔f1 ♗c8 33.h5 ♖ab7 34.♖h2 ♖a7 35.♔e1 ♖ab7 36.♔d1 ♖a7 37.♔c2 ♖ab7 38.♔b3 ♖a7 39.♕g3 ♖ab7 40.f4 exf4 41.♗xf4 ♖a7 42.♘d1 gxf5 43.exf5 ♘g7 44.♘e3 h6 45.f6 1-0

2. T. Petrosian – W. Unzicker

Hamburg 1960

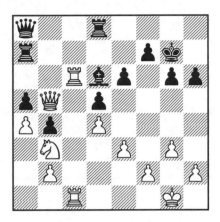

Here too, the game is a one-way street. White's pieces have literally stalemated Black; only the king is barely able to move. But what's strange is that this is still not enough for White to win: he can't see where to make the decisive incursion. Therefore, White prepares a kingside pawn storm, the goal being to break down the black king's pawn bastions. Just as in the preceding example, before undertaking the decisive action, he brings his king over to the opposing flank.

29.♔f1! ♔g8

If 29...♖b8, then 30.♖b6 ♖d8 31.♖cc6 with a decisive invasion.

30.h4 h5 31.♖1c2 ♔h7 32.♔e1 ♔g8 33.♔d1 ♔h7 34.♔c1 ♔g8 35.♔b1 ♔h7 36.♕e2 ♕b7 37.♖c1 ♔g7 38.♕b5! ♕a8

The variations following 38...♕xb5 all clearly favor White, e.g. 39.axb5 a4 40.b6 ♖ad7 (40...♖aa8 41.b7 ♖ab8 42.♘a5) 41.♘a5 ♖a8 42.♖xd6! ♖xd6 43.b7 ♖b8 44.♖c8 ♖d8 45.♖xd8 ♖xd8 46.♘c6.

39.f4 ♔h7

If 39...f5, then 40.♖b6 ♔f7 41.♖cc6.

40.♕e2 ♕b7 41.g4!

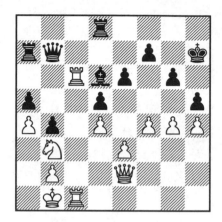

The decisive break.

41...hxg4 42.♕xg4 ♕e7 43.h5 ♕f6 44.♔a2!

Typical prophylaxis, helping White to avoid a queen trade.

44...♔g7 45.hxg6

45.♖g1 doesn't look bad, either.

45...♕xg6 46.♕h4 ♗e7

46...♖h8 allows the winning 47.♕f2.

47.♕f2 ♔f8 48.♘d2 ♖b7 49.♘b3 ♖a7 50.♕h2! ♗f6

50...♗d6 doesn't save Black: 51.♖xd6! ♖xd6 52.f5 exf5 53.♖c8+ ♔e7 54.♕h8 and wins.

51.♖c8! ♖ad7

In the variation 51...♖xc8 52.♖xc8+ ♔e7 53.f5 ♕xf5 54.♕b8 ♖d7, White mates with 55.♖e8.

52.♘c5! b3+

If 52...♖c8, then 53.♘xd7+ ♔e7 54.♖xc8; or if 52...♖d6, then 53.f5 ♕xf5 54.♕xd6+ with a decisive advantage in both cases.

53.♔xb3 ♖d6 54.f5! ♖b6+ 55.♔a2 1-0

It bears noting that *Fritz* 12 is generally unable to understand what the ninth world champion is up to by shifting the king to the opposite wing. There's only one point where it "agrees with" Petrosian – on White's move 44.

3. M. Botvinnik – P. Ostojić

Belgrade 1969

Knowing when to put off castling is a sure sign of how deeply a chessplayer understands the position.

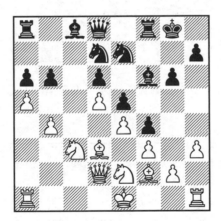

In the diagram position, Mikhail Botvinnik played...

17.♖a2

...not revealing yet where his king is headed. For on the king's wing, should he castle there, he could easily fall under the storming enemy pawns. His young opponent somewhat naively replied...

127

17...b5

Black has blocked up the queenside, so the experienced Botvinnik tucks his own king away on that now-safe wing before launching his own attack.

18.♔d1 ♖f7 19.♔c1 ♕c7 20.♔b1 ♕b7 21.♖c1 ♘f8 22.♗c2 ♗d7 23.♗b3 ♔g7 24.♖ac2 ♘g8 25.♘d1 ♗d8 26.♘b2 ♘f6 27.♘d3 ♘e8 28.h4! h6 29.♕d1 ♖c8 30.♕g1 ♖xc2 31.♖xc2 ♗c8 32.g3!

32...fxg3 33.♕xg3 ♘f6 34.♕g2 ♘h5 35.♘g3 ♘xg3 36.♕xg3 ♖c7 37.f4!

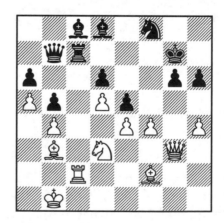

37...♖xc2 38.♗xc2 exf4 39.♗d4+ ♔h7 40.♕xf4 ♕e7 41.e5!

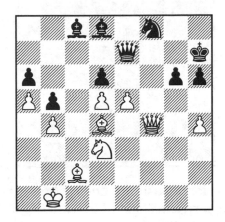

41...dxe5 42.♗xe5 ♘d7 43.♗b2 ♕f8 44.h5 ♕xf4 45.♘xf4 ♔g8 46.hxg6

A brilliant demonstration of pawn breaks (32.g3!, 37.f4!, 41.e5!). It's no accident that many outstanding chessplayers have carefully studied the games of Mikhail Botvinnik!

1-0

Truly we must marvel at how many brilliant examples there are on the theme of king play in the games of Tigran Petrosian and Anatoly Karpov. Let's show another game by the twelfth world champion.

4. A.H. Williams – A. Karpov

Nice Olympiad 1974

(see diagram next page)

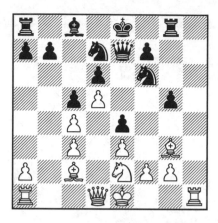

This is a rather closed position. Look at how masterfully Karpov prepares, and then executes, his plan with ...f7-f5-f4, while at the same time transferring the king to a safe zone.

15.♕b1 ♔d8 16.a4 a5! 17.♖a2 ♔c7 18.♖h6 ♖a6! 19.♕b5 ♔b8 20.♖b2 ♔a7 21.♕b3 ♘g4 22.♖h1 f5 23.♔d1 ♖b6 24.♕a2 ♖xb2 25.♕xb2 b6 26.♗b3 ♗a6 27.♘c1 ♘de5

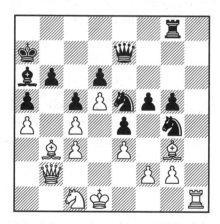

Compare the current position to the original one: all of Black's pieces are working and his king is completely safe. The time has come for decisive action.

28.♕e2 ♘g6 29.♔d2 ♘f6 30.♕d1 f4 0-1

Next, it's the ninth world champion at the board.

5. T. Petrosian – L. Ljubojević

Manila 1974

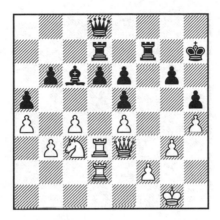

White has nailed his opponent down to the defense of the backward d6-pawn. But this pawn is not so easy to win. If we try attacking it with our queen, from d1 then Black plays his queen to f6, threatening White's f2-pawn, preventing White from removing the d6-pawn. As always, Petrosian finds something out of the ordinary. He decides on a kingside pawn storm, prefacing it by moving his king to a safe location.

50.♔f1! ♖f8 51.♔e1 ♕c7 52.♔d1 ♖f6 53.♔c2 ♕d8 54.f3 ♖ff7 55.♕g1 ♕c7 56.♔b2 ♖d8 57.♕d1 ♖fd7 58.g4!

The storm begins.

58...♔h8

Now let's observe the white queen's maneuvers.

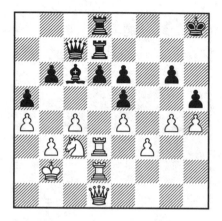

59.♕g1! ♖g7 60.♕e3! ♔h7 61.♕g5!

The decisive incursion!

61...♗e8 62.♕f6! ♖e7 63.gxh5 gxh5 64.♖g2! ♖dd7 65.♘b5 ♕c5 66.♖xd6! ♕e3 67.♘a3 ♕f4 68.♕xf4 exf4 69.♖xd7 ♗xd7

Now watch as the former world champion exploits his advantage in the technical phase.

70.c5!

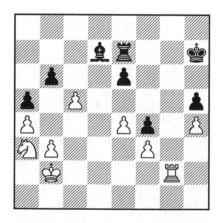

70...bxc5 71.♘c4 ♗c8 72.♖g5 ♔h6 73.♖xc5 ♗a6 74.♘e5 ♗e2 75.♖c2 ♗f1 76.♖c1 ♗e2 77.♖e1 ♗a6 78.♖g1 ♗e2 79.♔c2! ♔h7 80.♔d2

Driving the bishop away from its active position.

80...♗a6 81.♖g5 ♔h6 82.♖g8 ♗f1 83.♖g6+ ♔h7 84.♖g5 ♔h6 85.♖g1 ♗a6 86.♘c4 ♖c7 87.♔c3 ♖d7 88.♖g5 ♖d1 89.♖xa5 ♗xc4 90.♔xc4 ♖f1 91.♖e5 ♖xf3 92.♖xe6+ ♔g7 93.♖e5 ♖e3 94.♔b4 f3 95.♖f5 ♖xe4+ 96.♔a3 ♖e3 97.♖f4 ♔g6 98.♔b4 ♔g7 99.a5 ♔g6 100.♔a4 1-0

6. T. Petrosian – J. Peters

Lone Pine 1976

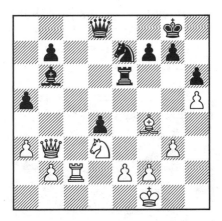

Indeed, it is hard to disagree with the prevailing opinion that there are similarities between the artistry of Petrosian and that of Karpov. It seems to me that both of them possess the unique ability to outplay their opponents from an equal position. The old-school masters who had this quality more than anyone else were clearly José Raúl Capablanca and Akiba Rubinstein.

In the present game, too, the position looks completely even; yet by some barely noticeable means, Black drifts into a lost position. Later, after the game, analysis showed that on one of his moves, Black might have held the position by playing something else. But in practice it's very hard to defend positions that are devoid of counterplay. Besides, both Petrosian and Karpov knew how to set problems for their opponents, while squeezing the maximum possible out of their position. This game bears witness to that.

34.♔e1 ♘d5 35.♕b5 ♘f6 36.♔d1 ♘d5 37.♗e5 ♘e7 38.g4 ♘c6 39.♗g3 ♘a7 40.♕b3 ♘c6 41.♔c1 ♖e4 42.f3 ♖e3 43.♔b1

White has executed the first part of his plan: to get his king out of danger before launching the decisive pawn storm. Here the computer recommends 43...♖e8 (or 43...♖e6); in both cases, it prefers White's position. Evidently, only the computer, with its ironclad play, has the strength to hold the position together in circumstances like this, which require the greatest technical skill. Human beings, on the other hand, are frequently known to make mistakes.

Black's next move doesn't lose; it's just that it gives Petrosian the opportunity to execute one of his favorite tricks: exchanging bishop for knight, leaving himself with a good knight against his opponent's (rather) weak bishop.

43...♘e7 44.♗h4! ♕d6 45.♗xe7

Fritz consigns this move to its "second line;" its top line is the complicated 45.g5. It's a good test on the theme of the differing approaches of machines and humans. A human chessplayer is more often influenced by his previous experience, while the machine always prefers the best move possible. Incidentally, you may have noticed that the machine sometimes "understands" the human's move later on, somewhat grudgingly altering its previous evaluation. Meanwhile, Petrosian follows his positional considerations, leaving himself the good knight versus Black's bad bishop. On top of that, with this exchange, Black's counterplay is reduced to practically nothing. Why drown oneself in a maelstrom of complicated variations, when there's something clear and simple instead?

45...♖xe7 46.♖c8+ ♔h7 47.♖f8 ♕c7 48.f4

Petrosian is true to himself. He does not deviate from the general plan. That said, the Fritzian 48.g5 would have ended the game right away.

48...♗c5?

Loses more quickly.

49.♕d5

49.♘xc5 ♕xc5 50.♕d3+ g6 51.♖xf7+ wins immediately.

49...♖e5 50.♖xf7

Here too, we see a difference between man and machine – the latter prefers to continue with 50.♘xe5 ♗xf8 51.g5. But, seeing that further resistance would be useless,

1-0

7. A. Karpov – U. Andersson

London 1984

In this game, played on first board in the match between the Soviet Union and the Rest of the World teams, Anatoly Karpov once again showed his extensive command of king play in a complex middlegame position. Remember that such a proactive relocation of one's most important piece is often possible in positions where the pawn structure is frozen – in other words, when there are no pawn breaks available to open up the game. Pay attention, too, to the fact of the king's return to the kingside following the knight trade. Here, before the center break, no doubt his position would be less endangered.

From an educational standpoint, it is notable how White executes pawn breaks with a further incursion. Compare this sort of play with Botvinnik's game with Ostojić (Game 3) earlier in this chapter.

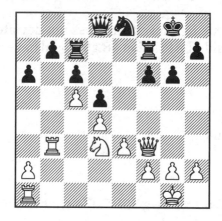

24.♔f1 ♘g7 25.♔e2 ♖ce7 26.♔d1 ♕c8 27.♖ab1 h5 28.h3 ♘e6 29.h4 ♔h7 30.♕h3 ♕e8 31.♔c2 ♖d7 32.♔b2 ♘g7 33.♘f4 ♖fe7 34.♔a1 ♕f7 35.♖g1 ♘e6 36.♘d3 ♘g7 37.g4!

37...hxg4 38.♖xg4 ♘h5 39.♖b1 ♕e6 40.♕f3 ♖g7 41.♖bg1 ♖de7 42.♔b2 ♔h6 43.♔c3 ♕f7 44.♘f4 ♘xf4 45.♖xf4 ♖e6 46.♔d2 ♕e7 47.♔e2 ♔h7 48.♔f1 ♔h6 49.♖g3 ♔h7 50.♖fg4 ♕f7 51.♖f4 ♔h6 52.♔g1 ♔h7 53.♔h2 ♔h6 54.♕g2 ♔h7 55. ♔g1 ♖e8 56.♕f3 ♖f8 57.♔f1 ♕e8 58.♕d1 ♕e8 59.♕b1 ♔h6 60.♔e2 ♕d8 61.♖fg4 ♖fg8 62.♔f1 ♕e8 63.♕d1 ♕e6 64.♕f3 ♖f7 65.♔g1 ♖fg7 66.a3 ♖e7 67.♔h2 ♖f7 68.♖f4 ♔h7 69.♕d1 ♔h6 70.♕d3 ♕e8 71.e4

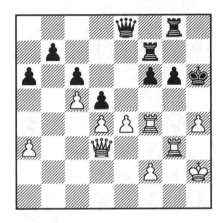

71...dxe4 72.♖xe4 ♕d7 73.♕e3+ ♔h7 74.♖e6 ♖gg7 75.♖f3 f5 76.h5

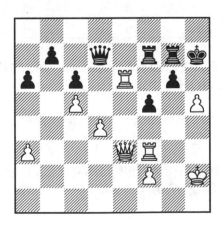

76...gxh5 77.♕h6+ ♔g8 78.♖fe3 ♕c7+ 79.♔h3 ♖e7 80.♖xe7 ♖xe7 81.♕g6+ ♔f8 82.♕f6+ ♔e8 83.♕h8+ ♔d7 84.♖xe7+ ♔xe7 85.♕g7+ 1-0

Samvel Ter-Sahakyan, the young Armenian grandmaster, is well acquainted with the intricacies of king play in complex middlegame and opening positions. See how easily he outplayed an experienced international master!

8. S. Ter-Sahakyan – J. Rukavina

Rijeka 2010

40.♔g1 ♗f8 41.♔f1 ♗h6 42.♔e1 ♔e7 43.♔d1 ♕f8 44.♔c2 ♘b8 45.♖dd1 ♘a6 46.♔b1

The evacuation is complete. Now it's time to prepare the pawn breaks.

46...♗f4 47.♘f1 ♗e8 48.g3 ♗h6 49.♘h2 ♗f7 50.♖dg1 ♕e8 51.♖g2 ♘b8 52.♖hg1 ♘d7 53.♔b2 ♖h7 54.f3

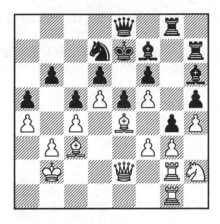

The first break!

54...gxf3 55.♘xf3 ♕f8 56.♘e1 ♕e8 57.♘c2 ♘b8 58.♘a3 ♘a6 59.♘b5 ♕b8 60.♗f3 ♘c7 61.♘a3 ♕c8 62.♘b1 ♗e8 63.♗e4 ♗d7 64.♖f1 ♗e8 65.♗e1 ♗f7 66.♘c3 ♕e8 67.♗f3 ♖hh8 68.♔b1 ♖h7 69.♘e4 ♖hh8 70.♗c3 ♘a6 71.♖fg1 ♘b8 72.♗b2 ♘a6 73.♘f2 ♘b8 74.♗c3 ♕c8 75.♗e4 ♘d7 76.♘d3 ♔d8 77.♗f3 ♗f8 78.♔b2 ♘b8 79.♕e4 ♘a6 80.♖e1 ♘c7 81. ♘f4! ♕d7 82.♘e6+ ♔c8 83.♖eg1 ♗h6 84.♕e2 ♕e8 85.♕f2 ♘a6 86.♕e1 ♔b7 87.♕e2 ♔a7 88.♗e1 ♔b7 89.g4

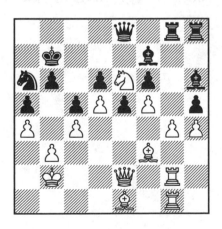

This is the second break – and it's the decisive one.

89...hxg4 90.♗xg4 ♔a7 91.♕f3 ♔b7 92.♖f1 ♘b8 93.♖fg1 ♔c8 94.h5 ♔b7 95.♕h3 ♘d7 96.♗e2 ♘f8 97.♗h4 ♘h7

Now comes the classic incursion!

98.♖g6!

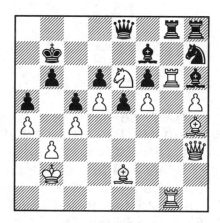

98...♘g5 99.♕g4 ♗xg6 100.fxg6 ♘xe6 101.dxe6 ♕e7 102.♕f3+ ♔c7 103.♕d5 ♗g7 104.♗f3 ♖b8 105.♕c6+ ♔d8 106.♖d1 1-0

Chapter 6

//

The King Protects Weaknesses

This aspect of king play involves taking the weak points in your own camp under control. Under the concept of "weak points" we include pawns as well as strategically significant empty squares. Note that, as in our preceding chapter about the evacuation of the king, *Fritz* 12 does not wholly accept this strategic technique.

1. B. Sliwa – M. Botvinnik

Maróczy Memorial, Budapest 1952

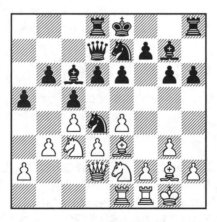

Earlier, Black had somewhat weakened his king's wing with ...h7-h6. Now it wouldn't be good for him to play either ...h6-h5 or ...g6-g5. Therefore, Botvinnik slides his king over to h7 in order to protect this weak spot.

16...♔f8! 17.♘f4 ♔g8 18.♘ce2 ♔h7

The objective is achieved. Now many people would prefer Black's game.

19.♗xd4 cxd4 20.b4 ♖a8

Evidently, he should prefer an open game on the queenside with 20...axb4.

21.b5 ♗b7 22.a4 ♖he8

22...♖hf8, preparing ...f7-f5, deserves consideration.

23.♗h3 ♘g8 24.♘c1 ♕d8 25.♘b3 h5 26.♕d1 ♘h6 27.♘e2 e5 28.f4 ♗c8 29.f5

After 29.♗xc8, White didn't like the fact that the black knight could land on e3. Evidently he believed that, in a closed position, Black wouldn't be able to exploit the power of his light-squared bishop. But now everything goes Black's way. Black skillfully outplays his opponent from a slightly superior position.

29...♘g4 30.♗xg4 hxg4 31.fxg6+ fxg6

Botvinnik did not like this move, preferring 31...♔xg6, intending to continue with ...f7-f5. *Fritz*, however, rates both moves more or less the same.

32.♔g2 ♖a7 33.♘g1 ♗h6 34.♘a1 ♖h8 35.♘c2 ♔g8 36.♖f2 ♖ah7 37.♕e2 ♗g5 38.♔h1 ♗f4 39.♖g2 ♗g5 40.♖f1 ♗e6 41.♖ff2 ♔g7 42.♕e1 ♖h5 43.♕e2 ♕e7 44.♖f1 ♔g8 45.♖ff2 ♕g7 46.♖f1 ♕h6 47.♖ff2 ♖h7 48.♖f1 ♗d7 49.♖ff2 ♗c8 50.♖f1 ♗e7 51.♖ff2 ♖f5!

Botvinnik skillfully takes over the f-file.

52.♖f1 ♖xf1 53.♕xf1 ♖f7 54.♕e1

If 54.♖f2, then 54...♖xf2 55.♕xf2 ♕c1. Now Black's major pieces invade the enemy camp with great effect, ensuring the victory.

54...♛f8 55.♖e2 ♖f1 56.♛d2 ♛f3+ 57.♖g2 ♖d1 58.♛h6 ♛f6

58...♖xg1+ also wins.

59.♖d2 ♝f8 60.♛xf8+ ♛xf8 61.♖xd1 ♛f2 62.♘e1 ♛b2 0-1

With good reason did so many outstanding players learn from the games of the sixth world champion!

2. N. Rashkovsky – L. Psakhis

Russian Chp, Volgograd 1977

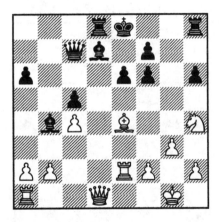

In this example, the pawns on f6 and h6 are weak. Black could castle, of course; but Black prefers to leave his rook where it is to defend the h-pawn, as well as the h7 square.

22...♚f8! 23.♛c2 ♚g7 24.♘g2

24.♖d1 is more natural.

24...f5 25.♝f3 ♝c6 26.♝xc6 ♛xc6 27.a3 ♝a5 28.b4 ♝c7 29.b5 ♛b7 30.a4 ♖d4

And here we have the first fruits: Black plants himself on the outpost.

31.♖b1 ♗a5! 32.♘f4 ♖hd8

Now Black has the better of it: he might just close up the queen's wing with ...a6-a5 and ...♗b4, rendering White's passed b-pawn worthless. It's not hard to envision Black's major pieces invading, either. But White, in a tough position, commits a decisive error and the game ends in a few short moves.

33.♖xe6?! ♖xf4 34.♕b2+ ♖fd4 35.♖xa6 ♕f3 36.♖f1 ♗c3 37.♕c1 ♖d2 38.♖c6 f4 0-1

3. N. Spiridonov – G. Kasparov

European Team Chp, Skara 1980

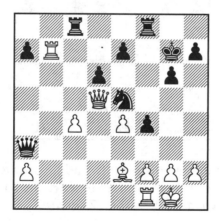

Black's strategic pluses in the position are indisputable: his "eternal" knight plus better pawn structure. But for the moment, he must resolve the problem he has with the e7-pawn. If he plays 20...♖f7, then 21.♕e6 will leave his pieces tied up. So, not only is the e7-pawn weak, but the e6 square as well.

20...♔f6!

With a single move, Garry Kasparov takes care of the problem! Meanwhile, *Fritz* plumps for 20...♖f7, and it's not embarrassed by the passive position that follows 21.♕e6 ♖e8, because it believes that White's initiative will be purely temporary, while the engine will pocket another pawn at a2.

21.h4

Worth a look is 21.♕d2 aiming at the f4-pawn, defending the a2-pawn, and freeing up the fifth rank for the rook. Now Kasparov manages to trade off the active white rook, exploiting his opponent's excessive sluggishness.

21...h6 22.♖d1

Again, 22.♕d2 is better.

22...♖b8 23.♖c7 ♖fc8 24.♖xc8 ♖xc8 25.♕b7 ♕c5

Consolidating. The simple-minded *Fritz*, on the other hand, prefers the mysterious rook move 25.....♖f8, in order to get the most out of the black queen.

26.♕b2 ♕b6 27.♕c1 g5 28.♖d5 e6 29.hxg5+ hxg5 30.♖d1 ♔e7!

Once again, the king protects a weak pawn – this time the one on d6!

31.♕c2 ♖b8 32.♕a4

The decisive mistake in a joyless position. Again, it was necessary to keep the queen at d2.

32...g4! 33.♕a3 ♕c5! 34.♕c3 g3 35.♖f1 gxf2+ 36.♖xf2 ♖b1+ 37.♗f1 ♕e3 38.♕xe3 fxe3 39.♖c2 ♘xc4 0-1

4. A. Karpov – G. Kasparov

World Chp (7), London/Leningrad 1986

A game fragment in which both sides make use of the method we're examining: taking weak squares under control. In addition, both kings assured their rooks' cooperation by refraining from castling.

15.♔f2 ♗f5 16.♗f1

Karpov uses an original strategic technique: he avoids exchanges when he has a space advantage. Now, what does *Fritz* do? It does not shy away from the trade; for, according to the computer, moving the bishop backwards cannot be good since, from the starting position, it controls fewer squares. Clearly, this all has a transient quality about it. This is the exact situation we can describe as one step back, two steps forward. Try explaining all of that to *Fritz*...

16...♔f8 17.♔g2 a5 18.a3 ♕d8 19.♘h3 ♗xh3+ 20.♔xh3 ♔g7 21.♔g2

The game continued:

21...♘d7 22.♗d3 ♘f8 23.♗e3 ♘e6 24.♘e2 ♘h6 25.b4

The position gets very complex after this move. White provokes Black into playing ...c6-c5, which results by force in a sharp change in the situation on the board. In a complicated tactical battle, Kasparov succeeds in outplaying his powerful opponent beautifully, but is unable to bring matters through to victory. One might easily agree with the computer's recommendation of 25.h4, with pressure.

25...♕b6 26.b5 c5 27.♘c3 cxd4 28.♗xh6+ ♖xh6 29.♘xd5 ♕d8 30.♗e4 h4 31.♖hf1 hxg3 32.hxg3 ♖c8 33.♖h1 ♖xh1 34.♖xh1 ♗g5! 35.f4 ♖c5!

Kasparov tries to change an unfavorable situation by energetic means.

36.fxg5

Here Karpov fails to withstand Black's powerful pressure, and passes on the strong move 36.♔g1 with the idea of doubling rooks on the h-file. But believe me, it's not so easy to find this idea when you're running low on time.

36...♖xd5 37.♗xd5 ♕xd5+ 38.♔h2 ♕xe5 39.♖f1 ♕xb5

39...♘xg5 is worth considering, either now or after a preliminary 39...a4.

40.♕f2! ♘xg5

This move, made just before the time control, costs Black the advantage. After 40...♕d7, he could still have fought for the win from a somewhat better position.

41.♕xd4+ ½-½

Draw!

This engrossing game, like so many other games of the 1985 and 1986 world championship matches, the reader may find annotated by Kasparov in his most interesting book, *Two Matches*. Highly recommended for strong chessplayers – study it carefully!

5. A. Petrosian – L. van Wely

Dortmund 1992

This book is about king play in complex positions in the middle-game and opening phases. Your author thought for a long time over whether to include the following position, since both queens are off the board. But, considering the complicated situation (for only the queens and one set of pawns are traded off, giving this position the character of a complex middlegame), we have decided to include it in this book since it presents the basic idea of this chapter in extremely sharp focus.

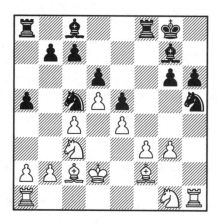

White has a significant space advantage; in addition, the queens are off the board, which in many King's Indian Defense positions favors White. But our experienced eye has already figured out White's basic problem – he has weak pawns at f3 and g3. I am confident that many readers will already have guessed how White solved this problem.

17.♔e2! ♗d7 18.♔f1! a4 19.♔g2!

For nitpicky readers, I wish to explain that the exclamation marks are for the idea more than for the strength of these moves. Other continuations are also possible, but this prophylaxis is a good example to emulate. At the same time, *Fritz* 12 suggests 17.g4 or 17.♘b5 at the start of the sequence above.

19...♖a5 20.♘ge2 ♖fa8 21.♗e1

Looks more like a psychological assault. The natural 21.♗e3 seems more solid.

21...c6

Logical, but a bit early.

22.♕b1

22.♖d1, taking aim at the weak pawn on d6, is worth considering.

22...♗f6?

But this is an error that White fails to exploit (22...♘f6 is more natural). Now White should play 23.g4.

23.b4

This has one significant drawback: it opens the file where Black's rooks will soon be deployed.

23...axb3 24.axb3 ♖a2!?

An interesting plan.

25.♘xa2 ♖xa2 26.♗xd1 cxd5 27.♔f1!

GM Arshak Petrosian displays fine positional understanding. Of course, not for nothing does he have the same last name as the ninth world champion!

27...d4

27...dxc4 looks stronger.

28.♘c1!?

A picturesque position! White's entire army is posted along the first rank. But this is just a brief pause prior to the decisive push forward. Played Nimzowitsch-style (and human-style, too)! Now the computer prefers the more forceful 28.g4!.

28...♖a8 29.b4 ♘e6 30.♘d3 ♔g7 31.♖h2 ♘g5 32.♖d2 ♖a3 33.♔g2

This dovetails with our theme, although it would have been more accurate to consolidate with 33.♗e2. Even the most attractive idea needs to be executed at the right time.

33...♘e6

Fritz's recommendation of 33...♗h3+ and – on any king move – 34...♗e6, with a beautiful position, is worth considering. Now the contest comes quickly to an end.

34.♗b3 ♗a4 35.♗xa4 ♖xa4 36.c5

36.♖dd1 is good.

36...罝a3 37.cxd6 含f7

37...罝xd3 doesn't help matters.

38.勺c5 勺g5 39.罝b3 罝a1 40.亼f2 b6 41.勺d7 b5 42.勺c5 勺e6 43.罝bb2 亼g5 44.罝a2 1-0

6. E. Danielian – A. Segal

European Jr (Girls) Chp, Litomyšl 1994

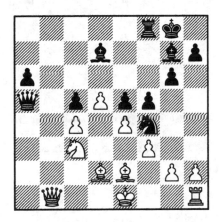

White has some impressive positional pluses, including a harmonious pawn chain headed by the passed d-pawn; while Black's pawns at a6, c5, and even e5 can hardly brighten her position. Therefore Black, in the coming struggle, will pin all her hopes on activating her pieces.

24.含f2

Not only establishing communication between her heavy pieces, but also defending the g2-pawn. Another possibility is 24.亼f1.

24...亼h6 25.豐b2

25.豐c2, avoiding 25...豐b4, is a little better.

25...♘xe2?!

Somewhat clichéd, the idea being to exploit the position of the white king. Now the king will find a fairly comfortable spot in the center. As we have said before, 25...♕b4 didn't look bad.

26.♔xe2 ♗xd2 27.♕xd2 ♕b4

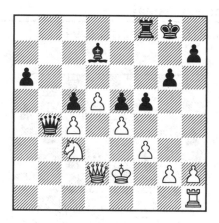

28.♔d3!

Protecting the weak pawn.

28...♗a4 29.♘xa4

White might also have quietly won a pawn with 29.♕a2 ♗b3 30.♕xa6, without a shred of compensation for her opponent.

29...♕xa4 30.♕b2 fxe4+ 31.fxe4 ♕d7

31...♕e8 would meet with 32.♕b7.

32.♕xe5 ♖e8 33.♕f6 ♕b7 34.♖e1 a5 35.♕c3 a4 36.e5 ♕e7 37.e6 ♖b8 38.♕e5

Black resigned a few moves later.

7. B. Ivanović – E. Sveshnikov

USSR–Yugoslavia
Krk 1976

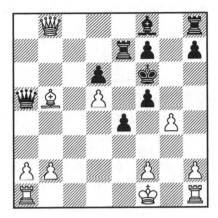

Black's weak pawn may be defended in one of two ways: 22... ♕b4 (objectively the stronger line) or the text move below. The latter choice would certainly be the less expected one: king in the absolute center of the board! So White resolves to punish his opponent immediately – for which action he gets punished himself. This is the kind of shock that can be caused to one's opponent by such a king move!

22...♔e5!? 23.f4+

The engine suggests 23.♗e2 or 23.♗c4, with slightly better play for White. But in this case we consider the engine's evaluation to be of less importance. It would seem to us that, in these types of positions, knowing how to play them would carry greater weight.

23...♔xf4!

Black is playing as though he has ice in his veins. One unusual-looking line might be 24.♕xd6+ ♖e5!. This would be White's most accurate line, even though Black would still have the better of it.

Evidently, though, such original play by Black knocked Ivanović clean out of his senses, and he loses without a fight.

24.♔e2 ♔e5!

The king has done what he came for; now it's time for him to go home!

25.♖hf1 fxg4!

Again, very strongly played!

26.b4! ♗g7!

Avoiding one final trap – 26...♕xb4? 27.♖f5+! and it is White who wins: in one line he mates; in the other, he wins the queen. 26...♕a3 was very strong, too.

27.bxa5 ♖xb8 28.♖ab1 f5 29.a6 f4 30.♗c6 f3+ 31.♔f2 ♖xb1 32.♖xb1 ♔f4! 33.♖b4 ♗c3 34.♖c4 ♗a5 35.♔f1 ♗b6 36.♗b7 h5 37.♖c6 e3 38.♖c4+ ♔g5 0-1

8. A. Shirov – G. Kasparov

Tilburg 1997

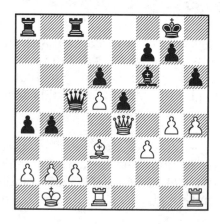

First the black king gets out of the danger zone – *à la* Steinitz – since on 22...a3 White has the prosaic reply 23.g5 hxg5 24.hxg5 ♗xg5 25.♖h8+, mating.

22...♔f8 23.g5

What else is there? If 23.♖dg1, then 23...♗xh4.

23...hxg5 24.hxg5 ♗xg5 25.♕f5

He needed to send the rook to h7.

25...♗h6 26.♖h4

Now, the most interesting part begins!

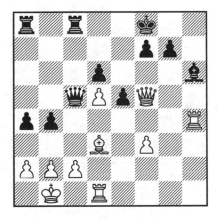

26...♔e7!

The king defends both weaknesses, d6 and f7. And – most amazing – the then-world champion offers a positional queen sacrifice! Afterward, White will find it hard to play his game, as he will have no plan, while Black risks nothing.

27.♖c4 ♕xc4! 28.♗xc4 ♖xc4 29.♕d3 ♖ac8 30.♖e1 ♗f4 31.♖e4 ♖xe4 32.fxe4

If 32.♕xe4, then 32...♖h8.

32...g5 33.a3 bxa3 34.♕a6

White does everything he can to give his queen room to roam. He succeeds in this – but there's a surprise waiting for him!

34...♖d8 35.♕b6 g4 36.c4?

Loses prettily, whereas the simple 36.bxa3 would have left him with saving chances.

36...g3 37.c5 g2 38.cxd6+ ♖xd6 39.♕c7+

39...♔f6!!

Brilliantly played!

40.♕xd6+ ♔g7 0-1

Chapter 7

//

The King Facilitates Major-Piece Coordination

As a rule, castling is needed to coordinate our major pieces. But castling is impractical in certain situations. In such cases, a simple king move may establish the desired coordination.

Game 7 below, where the king helps its rook into the game, brings us sheer delight. The other examples are original, too – especially Games 4 and 11.

Note that the king most often assures cooperation between the minor pieces. This happens quite often in practice, and I think it deserves special consideration. One variation of the Slav Defense (which we mentioned in Chapter 3) is permeated with Steinitz's idea: White gives up castling for a material advantage, then his king embarks on a journey through almost the whole queenside – generally, with some success. I don't think that this would be the only example of this. One can find many similar cases in opening theory.

Interestingly, this tactical technique is not unknown to *Fritz* 12; and quite often, the program suggests the move the player actually made.

1. G. Ravinsky – A. Kotov

Leningrad 1949

(see diagram next page)

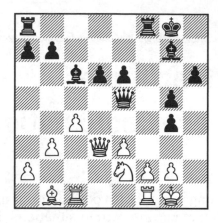

This game fragment is unique in that it combines several things we know about using the king in the middlegame: 1) the king protects itself by moving out of the danger zone; 2) the king defends weak spots in its own camp (in this case, the d6-pawn); and 3) the king helps to link up the major pieces. When the king moves back, the rooks gain access to the h-file. In connection with this, Black's kingside pawn storm becomes possible, with a dangerous attack. To *Fritz*'s credit, it too sees this king maneuver as optimal.

23...♔f7!! 24.♘g3 ♔e7 25.♕e2 h5! 26.♘xh5 ♖h8 27.♕xg4 ♖xh5! 28.♕xh5 ♖h8 29.♗h7 ♗e4 30.f4 ♕b2

With a queen sacrifice, White attempts to set up the semblance of a fortress.

31.♕xg5+ ♗f6 32.♕xf6+ ♔xf6 33.♗xe4 ♕xa2 34.♖b1 ♕d2 35.♖fe1 b6 36.♖bd1 ♕c3

Black's energetic play is impressive, but 36...♕b4, using the queen to protect the pawn, might have been stronger. Now White succeeds in activating his pieces.

37.♔f2 ♖d8?! 38.♖h1 ♖g8 39.♖h6+?!

After 39.g3 ♔e7 40.♖d4! ♖g7 41.♖d3, White could have fought for the draw.

39...♔e7 40.♖h7+ ♖g7 41.♖xg7+ ♕xg7 42.♖h1

Excessive activity leads to quick defeat. 42.♖b1 or 42.♖d4 holds out for longer.

42...♕b2+ 43.♔f3 a5

43...♕xb3 is simpler.

44.♖h7+

Again, White pins his hopes on activity, but the queen proves to be stronger. 44.♖b1 is necessary.

44...♔f8 45.g4 ♕xb3 46.g5 ♕xc4 47.♖a7 ♕f1+ 48.♔g4 ♕e2+ 49.♔h4 d5 50.♗h7 ♕xe3 51.♔g4 ♕e2+ 52.♔g3 b5 53.♖b7 d4 54.♖d7 ♔e8 0-1

2. Y. Averbakh – O. Panno

Buenos Aires 1954

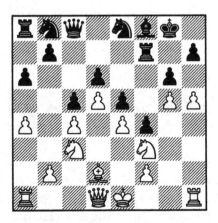

We want to note that White is playing his own variation – the Averbakh Variation – against the King's Indian Defense. He has outstripped Black to a considerable extent in developing his initiative. Instead of active kingside counterplay, Black has been relegated to a passive defense. White is also better in other sectors of the board. Before opening the h-file, GM Yuri Averbakh ensures the cooperation of his major pieces.

17.♔e2 ♖g7 18.♖h4 ♘d7 19.hxg6 hxg6 20.♕h1 ♗e7 21. ♖h8+ ♔f7 22.♕h6

First, the invasion.

22...♘f8 23.♖h1 ♖b8

The position is now ripe for a combination.

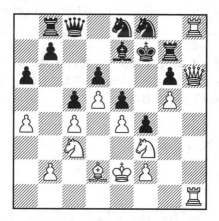

24.♗xf4!

And now, the destructive sacrifice.

24...♕c7 25.♕h2 ♘d7 26.♕h3 ♘f8 27.♖xf8+! ♔xf8 28.♕e6 ♖g8 29.♘h4 ♗d8 30.♘xg6+ ♔g7 31.♘xe5 1-0

This attack was executed according to all the rules of tactics! I don't think that, even among younger players, there is one who hasn't heard of Yuri Averbakh, a gifted chess theoretician, not just in the opening, but also in the endgame. He has written excellent theoretical works about all manner of endings. And his strength as a player is made clear when I say that Averbakh in his time became champion of the USSR, which was then the strongest chess country in the world!

3. J. Bednarski – T. Petrosian

Lugano Olympiad 1968

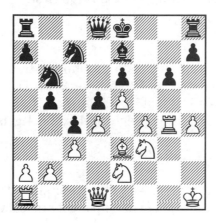

Black is for choice despite White's space advantage (the e5-pawn), since the classical solution for the current kingside pawn structure (h4-h5, and on ...g6xh5, preparation for, and execution of, f4-f5) would undoubtedly run into serious difficulties. Black is not forced to take on h5, and White's monarch might also suffer from opening up the position (as happened in the game).

16...♔d7!

Now Black's major pieces are connected along the eighth rank. The same thing would have occurred had Black castled, but in that case White's pawn breaks (b2-b3 and a2-a4) would have come in with greater effect. Now those breaks are not as strong thanks to Black's a8-rook. Besides, on d7, the king is safer now. *Fritz* 12 approves of the king maneuver.

17.♕c2 ♕f8 18.♖ag1 ♘e8

Improving the knight's placement: it's heading for f5. 18...♕f5 also looks decent.

19.♖4g2 ♘g7 20.♘g3 ♕f7 21.h5

Sticking with the program. White overestimates his chances. Perhaps he should throw in 21.♘g5 ♕g8 first.

21...♖af8 22.hxg6

Played hastily; this only pours gasoline on the flames. He should stick to a waiting strategy (22.♗d2 or 22.♗c1), or else go for the variation 22.h6 ♘f5 23.♘xf5 ♕xf5 24.♕xf5 ♖xf5 25.♘g5, although both lines give Black a small edge. As it is, Black gets more than that.

22...hxg6+ 23.♖h2 g5!

White evidently overlooked this possibility. The then-reigning world champion brings about his opponent's defeat with forceful play.

24.♖xh8 ♖xh8+ 25.♘h2 gxf4 26.♖f1 ♗g5 27.♕f2 ♘f5!

The conclusion of the knight's journey (c7-e8-g7-f5) is the final leg of the forcing maneuver Black began on move 23.

28.♘xf5 fxe3 29.♕g2 e2! 0-1

4. N. Razvalaev – A. Kalikshteyn

Tashkent 1972

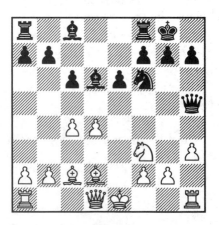

White wants to play 1.g4; but the h1-rook is undefended: Black would take the overzealous pawn with his knight. White handles this task brilliantly.

1.♔e2!

Now Black must sacrifice a minor piece in order to save his queen, without any compensation whatever.

1...e5 2.g4 ♗xg4 3.hxg4 ♕xg4 4.♕g1! ♕e6 5.♖xh7!

White proceeds in inspired fashion! The simple 5.d5 leads to the same result; but the text move is both strong and artistically pleasing!

5...exd4+ ♗e3 ♘xh7

Nor do other moves save Black.

7.♗xh7+ ♔h8 8.♕h1 g6 9.♗xg6+ ♔g7 10.♕h6+ ♔f6 11.♗f5+

Compare this episode with the fragment from Karpov–Kamsky (10...♔e7) in this same chapter!

1-0

5. V. Kovačević – Y. Seirawan

Wijk aan Zee 1980

(see diagram next page)

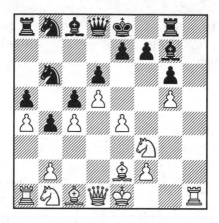

It's hard to believe that, after a mere 10-15 moves, Black's major pieces will dominate all the key files.

14...♔d7

The first step towards coordination.

15.♘bd2

White, having a stable space advantage, cannot copy Black with 15.♔d2 or 15.♗d3 with ♔e2 to follow, in view of his completely undeveloped queenside.

15...♖h8 16.♖g1 ♔c7 17.♖b1 ♖h3 18.b3 ♕h8

The second step...

19.♘f1 ♘8d7 20.♗f4 ♘e5 21.♘xe5 ♗xe5 22.♗xe5 ♕xe5 23.f3 ♗d7 24.♕c2 ♕d4 25.♖g2 ♖h1 26.♖f2 ♕h8 27.f4 ♕h4 28.♖d1 f6 29.gxf6 exf6 30.e5 fxe5 31.fxe5 ♖f8

Finally, the third and decisive step!

32.exd6+ ♔b7 33.♗d3 ♖e8+ 0-1

6. G. Kasparov – A. Karpov

World Chp (21), Moscow 1985

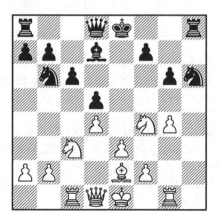

16.♔d2! ♕e7 17.b3

17.♔c2 is worth considering; now Black can try to get at the b3-pawn with 18...a5!?.

17...g5 18.♘d3 0-0-0 19.♖h1 f6 20.♕g1 ♘f7 21.♕g3 ♕d6 22.♕xd6 ♘xd6 23.f3

In this war of maneuver, White has managed to gain a small but secure advantage. Once again, your author recommends a careful study of Garry Kasparov's *Two Matches,* where you will find a lot of interesting and instructive material – and not just from this game. We wish just briefly to highlight this encounter's most engrossing moments.

23...♖dg8 24.♘c5 ♔d8 25.♗d3 ♗c8 26.♘e2 ♘a8 27.♗h7

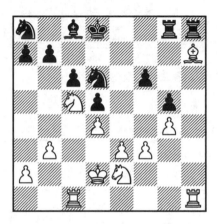

One of Anatoly Karpov's favorite techniques – carried out by Kasparov! Who could forget Karpov's game against the German GM Wolfgang Unzicker?

The point of this maneuver is to block the file so as to double the rooks, and then to invade. In this game, White did not succeed in taking over the h-file, as Karpov neutralized the incursion. But White did get a beautiful pawn center, and at one point he had a very attractive position.

27...♖f8 28.♖h6 ♘c7 29.♘g3 ♘f7 30.♖h2 ♘e6 31.♘d3 ♘g7 32.♖ch1 ♔e7 33.♘f2 ♖d8 34.♗f5 ♖xh2 35.♖xh2 ♘xf5 36.gxf5 ♖h8 37.♖xh8 ♘xh8 38.e4 ♘f7 39.♘g4 ♘d6 40.♘e3 dxe4 41.fxe4 b6 42.b4 ♗a6 43.♘g4 ♘b5 44.♔d3 ♘a3+ ½-½

Now we review that game, Karpov–Unzicker:

A. Karpov – W. Unzicker

Nice Olympiad 1974

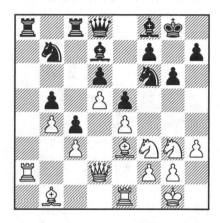

24.♗a7! ♘e8 25.♗c2 ♘c7 26.♖ea1 ♕e7 27.♗b1 ♗e8 28.♘e2 ♘d8 29.♘h2 ♗g7 30.f4 f6 31.f5 g5 32.♗c2 ♗f7 33.♘g3 ♘b7 34.♗d1 h6 35.♗h5 ♕e8 36.♕d1 ♘d8 37.♖a3 ♔f8 38.♖1a2 ♔g8 39.♘g4 ♔f8 40.♘e3 ♔g8 41.♗xf7+ ♘xf7 42.♕h5 ♘d8 43.♕g6 ♔h8 44.♘h5 1-0

7. L. Oll – J. Hodgson

PCA Qualifier, Groningen 1993

The following example is a real treat. Black's position is for preference, since his knight is better than White's bishop; additionally, queen plus knight is stronger than queen plus bishop. Note also that White lacks any constructive ideas. Yet all this is not enough to break down White's defenses. The problem is that the black rook is cut off from its army, and without it Black cannot hope to win. It seems Black lacks the wherewithal to solve this task. But Julian Hodgson comes through with flying colors. The Englishman succeeds in finding a most original path for the rook, retrieving it from solitary confinement and getting to join the rest of its troops. Indeed, there are no bounds to the human imagination – bravo, GM Hodgson! This kind of maneuver is usually seen only in chess compositions, where one piece opens up a path for another. We find it hard to present further examples from practical play. And may the reader forgive me – but I just can't resist decorating Black's moves with exclamation marks whenever they illustrate the above theme.

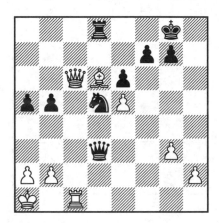

34...♔h7!! 35.♕c5 ♔g6! 36.h4 ♖h8! 37.a3

Here White could play 37.♕c2 – just as he might have on move 34; although there, too, Black would hold the upper hand. While on 37.♕f2, Black would reply 37...♖c8!. Objectively speaking, White's position isn't lost yet; but as we have noted already, it's so difficult to play a position where there is no exact plan of play, nor counterplay. Only many hours' worth of analysis could find the right answer here.

37...♖h5! 38.♕g1 ♔h7

38...♖f5 is more consistent, not allowing White the chance to get his queen to a7. After the game move, 39.g4 looks interesting, in order to meet the rook's capturing on h4 with 40.♕f2.

39.♖d1 ♕b3 40.♖d2 ♖f5!

Finally!

41.g4 ♖f4 42.♕b1+ ♔g8 43.g5

43.♖c2 runs into 43...♖c4 44.♖xc4 ♕xc4, with excellent winning chances.

43...b4 44.♖d3

Here it is – the decisive error in a bad position.

44...♘c3! 45.axb4

On 45.bxc3, 45...♕xa3+ 46.♕a2 ♖f1+ decides.

45...♕a2+

There are other, simpler wins too; but Hodgson rightly chooses the prettiest. A worthy finish to a brilliant phase of the game!

46.♕xa2 ♖f1+ 0-1

To conclude, I want to present an example from the field of chess problems on the theme of line clearance.

F. Gigli
1861

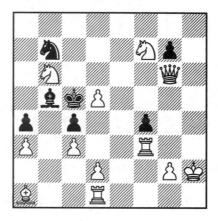

Mate in 3

1.♖h1!! ♗d7 2.♕b1 ♗b5 3.♕g1#

International Master Ashot Nadanian is one of those rare players who have managed to offer the chess world a new variation – in the Grünfeld Defense, and on move 5 at that!

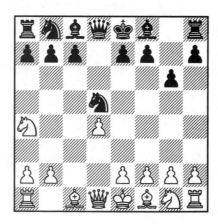

White has just played 5.♘c3-a4, avoiding the trade and preparing e2-e4. At the same time, from the a4 square, the knight restrains Black's standard thrust with ...c7-c5. This is how the Nadanian Variation starts out.

IM Nadanian is at once a practical player and a researcher. He also composes brilliant studies and problems. He has put together a unique collection of positions from games, as well as a collection of rare studies and problems. Every one of our conversations on chess themes gives me genuine pleasure.

We present a fragment from one of his games, with comments by the winner.

8. A. Nadanian – A. Tran

Singapore 2005

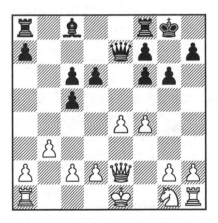

This move not only facilitates cooperation among the major pieces, but now His Majesty lives in absolute safety.

Extended over-the-board analysis convinced White to make this move, as he was uncomfortable with the lines where White tried to castle on either wing:

12.0-0-0? a5 13.a4 ♖e8 14.♖e1 ♖b8 15.d3 c4!! with a clear advantage for Black;

12.♘f3? ♖e8 13.d3 d5 14.♘d2 c4!! (14...♗f5?! 15.0-0 dxe4 16.♖ae1; 14...dxe4?! 15.dxe4 ♗f5 16.0-0-0, with approximate equality) 15.dxc4 (15.bxc4 dxe4 16.♘xe4 ♗f5, with good prospects) 15...♗f5 16.cxd5 cxd5 17.0-0 ♖ac8 18.c4 ♕c5+ 19.♔h1 dxe4, with an even game.

12.♔f2 ♖e8 13.♖e1 a5

If 13...f5, then 14.e5.

14.a4!

If 14.♘f3?!, then 14...a4 is equal.

14...♖b8 15.d3 ♖b4

15...c4 offers nothing due to 16.bxc4 ♖b4 17.♘f3 ♗g4 (17...♖xa4 18.♖a1!) 18.c3! ♕a7+ (18...♖a4? 19.♕c2, trapping the rook) 19.♕e3 ♕xe3+ 20.♔xe3 ♖xa4 21.♖a1, with a promising ending for White.

16.♘f3 ♕a7

Instead of this tempting move, 16...f5!? is worth considering.

17.♔g3! f5 18.♕d2!

If 18.e5, then 18...f6.

18...fxe4 19.♖xe4 ♖exe4?

19...♗e6 is better; although in that case White would still be on top.

20.dxe4 ♕d7

20...♖xe4 21.♕xd6 is also good for White.

21.♖d1!

White's advantage is close to decisive.

21...d5

Nor does 21...♖xe4 22.♕xd6 ♕g4+ 23.♔f2 save him.

22.exd5 cxd5 23.♕xd5 ♕g4+ 24.♔f2 ♗b7 25.♕e5 ♖d4 26.♕b8+ ♔g7 27.♖xd4 ♗xf3 28.♕e5+ f6 29.♕e7+ ♔h6 30. ♕f8+ ♔h5 31.♕xc5+ 1-0

9. S. Galdunts – H. Dolmazian

Yerevan 1988
Larsen's Opening A01

1.b3 e5 2.♗b2 ♘c6 3.c3 f5 4.♗b5 d6 5.f4 exf4 6.♕h5+! g6 7.♕e2 ♘f6 8.exf4+

Black has played this opening too fancifully, and now he has a difficult choice to make.

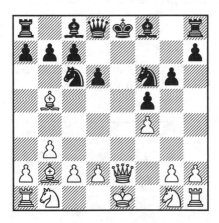

8...♔d7

A non-standard decision. Black doesn't want to have his king facing the crossfire of White's bishop pair after the objectively stronger 8...♔f7. As the Armenian player Haik Dolmazian put it, he understood that his choice of move was not the strongest; but during the battle, sometimes a player will be guided by psychological considerations. Now all that remains for Black to do is "only" to complete his development and secure the cooperation of his heavy artillery. Truthfully, it won't be so easy for White to refute Black's somewhat artificial play, either.

9.♘f3 ♗g7 10.0-0 a6 11.♗xc6+ bxc6

11...♔xc6 looks cute here – and it's not so bad, either.

12.♕d3 ♗b7 13.♘a3

13.♘e5+!? ♔e8 14.♘c4 looks interesting for White.

13...♕g8!

Black is trying to link up his two rooks.

14.♖fe1 ♕d5 15.♕f1 ♖he8!

Now Black's major pieces are connected.

16.c4 ♕g8

Compare the two diagrams above. Black has resolved all of his opening problems before White has.

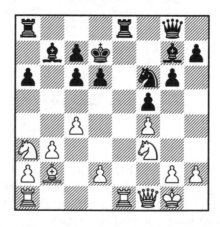

17.♘c2

17.c5!? is worth considering.

17...♖e4?!

Trying too hard: 17...c5 at once is better.

18.d3 ♖xe1 19.♖xe1 c5 20.b4

Evidently, he ought to have chosen 20.a3, preparing 21.b4. That would have left White's pawn chain looking more attractive; whereas now the play evens out.

20...cxb4 21.♘xb4 ♖e8 22.♖e2 ♘h5!?

Black makes no secret of wishing to exploit his opponent's lack of a light-squared bishop, since 23.g3 is now out of the question.

23.♖xe8 ♕xe8 24.♗xg7 ♘xg7 25.♘c2 ♘h5

25...♗xf3 26.♕xf3 ♕b8, with a dangerous initiative, looks very tempting.

26.♘d2 ♕e7 27.♕f2 ♘f6

An interesting struggle might have followed on 27...g5 28.fxg5 ♕xg5 29.♘e1 ♘f4 30.♔f1 c5 31.♘df3, with an approximately equal game. Black prefers to hold on to his superior pawn structure.

28.♕e3!?

Secures Black the better endgame.

28...♕xe3+ 29.♘xe3 d5

He might also have prepared for this break after 29...c5. One thing is clear already: Black is playing for the win. And one other thing is clear: in the ending, Black will have the better of it – thanks to the central placement of his king!

30.c5

White faces a difficult choice, so it won't be that hard for him to make a mistake. The "computer move" 30.♘b3 might be better.

30...d4 31.♘ec4

The variation 31.♘c2 ♗d5 32.♘xd4 ♗xa2 33.♘2f3 a5 34.♘e5+ ♔c8 also favors Black. Soon, Black will be outplaying White in the middle of the board. Undoubtedly, careful analysis with a chess engine will probably show some acceptable variation, but practical chessplayers know well how difficult it is to play positions like White's and avoid making a mistake.

31...♘d5 32.g3 ♘b4 33.♘e5+ ♔e6 34.a3 ♘c6 35.♘ec4 a5 36.a4 ♔d5 37.♘b3 ♗a6 38.♘b2 ♘b4 39.♘c1 ♔xc5 40.♘b3+ ♔d5 0-1

In conclusion, we return once again to the work of Anatoly Karpov. First, we present part of his game against Gata Kamsky:

10. G. Kamsky – A. Karpov

Dortmund 1993

In this familiar variation of the Caro-Kann, Karpov unexpectedly and drastically changed the situation on the board with his eleventh move. Certainly, after careful analysis with the help of our silicon friend *Fritz* it's easy to come up with evaluations and recommendations. But in practical play, matters will not go so smoothly. I should note that even so experienced a grandmaster as Kamsky was unable to refute Black's cheeky king move. The game has been carefully dissected and annotated by many grandmasters, so we present it without commentary.

(see diagram next page)

11...♔e7!

Played in the style of the old Steinitz (see Chapter 8). Karpov's idea reminds us of Game 4 in this chapter.

The move deserves its exclamation mark, because it sharply alters the course of the game, when coming to the forefront will be a player's understanding of how to act in non-standard situations. A brave choice!

The coordination of the major pieces along the eighth rank gives rise to mind-numbing complications. The threat of ...g7-g5 arises; play swings sharply into the realm of tactics, where Karpov's mastery becomes clear.

12.♘e5 ♗xe5 13.dxe5 ♕a5+ 14.c3 ♕xe5+ 15.♗e3 b6 16.0-0-0 g5 17.♕a4 c5 18.♖he1 ♗d7 19.♕a3 ♖hd8 20.g3 ♕c7 21.♗d4 ♗e8 22.♔b1 ♖d5 23.f4 ♖ad8 24.♗c2 ♖5d6 25.♗xf6+ ♔xf6 26.fxg5+ hxg5 27.♖xd6 ♖xd6 28.c4 ♔e7 29.♕e3 f6 30.h4 gxh4 31.gxh4 ♕d7 32.♕h6 e5 33.h5 ♕g4 34.♕h7+ ♔d8 35.h6 ♖d2 36.♕f5 ♕xf5 37.♗xf5 ♗d7 38.♗g6 ♖h2 39.h7 ♔e7 40.♗d3 ♗e6 41.♖g1 f5 42.♖g7+ ♔f6 43.♖xa7 e4 44.♗e2

f4 45.b3 f3 46.♗d1 ♗f5 47.♔c1 ♗xh7 48.♖b7 ♔e5 49.♖xb6 ♖xa2 0-1

I dearly love the following game. It's simply a pleasure to watch Anatoly Karpov's virtuoso handling of the king!

11. G. Kamsky – A. Karpov

Linares 1991

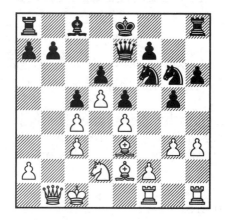

18...♔d8

Played as per our theme.

19.♘f3 ♔c7 20.h4 g4 21.♘e1 ♘h5 22.♕c2 ♕e8 23.♗d3 ♗d7 24.♕d2 ♕f8 25.♘c2 ♕g7 26.♔b2 ♖af8 27.♘a3 a6 28.♔a1 b6 29.♖b1 ♖b8 30.♖b3 ♘e7 31.♖hb1 ♕g6 32.♕b2 ♘c8 33.♘c2 ♘g7 34.♕a3 a5 35.♕c1 f5

The long-awaited breakthrough.

36.exf5 ♗xf5 37.♗xf5 ♘xf5 38.♗d2 ♖f8 39.♘a3 ♖b7 40.♖3b2 ♖f6 41.♕d1 ♔d8

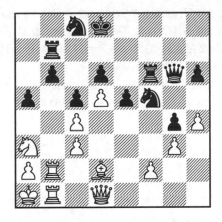

Once again, the king works to ensure cooperation among the major pieces.

42.♕a4 ♘fe7 43.♗e3 ♖f3 44.♘c2 ♖f6 45.♘e1 ♕e4 46.♖d1 ♖c7 47.♕b5 ♘f5 48.♗c1 ♔e7

Now, before doubling rooks on the f-file, Black evacuates his king to the safer king's wing.

49.♕a4 ♔f7 50.♘d3 ♘g7 51.♘e1 ♔g8 52.♗e3 ♖cf7 53.♕c6 ♖f8 54.♕a4 ♘f5 55.♗c1 ♖6f7 56.♘d3 ♔g7 57.♘e1 ♖f6 58.♕d7+

Allowing a pawn-winning fork.

58...♘fe7 59.♘d3 ♕xc4 60.♘xe5

White's clever counterplay comes to nothing; Black defends successfully and throws back the enemy forces.

60...dxe5 61.d6 ♖8f7 62.dxe7 ♘xe7 63.♕d2 ♖e6 64.♕e1 e4! 65.♖bd2 ♘c6 66.♖e2 ♖f3 67.♖d7+ ♔f8

And now Karpov uses the king to push out the active white rook! How many roles have been assigned to the king in this interesting game!

68.♗e3 ♔e8 69.♖b7 ♘e5 70.♖b2 ♘d3 71.♕d2 ♖ff6 72.♖b1 ♖d6 73.♕c2 a4 74.a3 ♔d8 75.h5 ♔c8 76.♖a7 b5 77.♖g7 b4 78.♖d1 b3 79.♕e2 ♘e5 80.♕e1 ♖xd1+ 81.♕xd1 ♖d6 82.♖g8+ ♔c7 83.♖g7+ ♔c6 84.♕c1

Truly, the king is a strong piece... in the right hands, that is!

Bravo, king!

0-1

12. I. Nepomniachtchi – A. Grischuk

Dagomys 2010
Sicilian Defense B90

1.e4 c5 2.♘f3 d6 3.d4 cxd4 4.♘xd4 ♘f6 5.♘c3 a6 6.h3 ♘c6 7.♗e3 e5 8.♘f3 ♗e7 9.g4 ♗e6 10.♘g5 h6 11.♘xe6 fxe6 12.♗c4 ♕d7 13.h4 b5 14.♗d3 ♘d4 15.♖g1 g5 16.♖h1 ♖f8 17.hxg5 hxg5 18.a3 ♕b7 19.♖h3

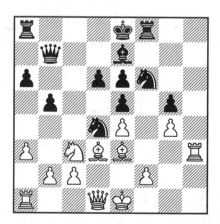

After a hard-fought opening, the players arrived at the diagram position.

19...♔d7 20.♔d2 ♖f7 21.f3 ♖af8 22.♘e2 ♘c6 23.c3 ♘e8 24.♕h1 ♘a5 25.♖d1 ♘c4+ 26.♗xc4 bxc4 27.♔c1

This position deserves its own diagram:

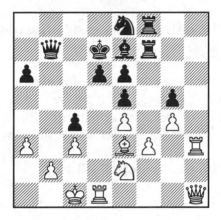

The king has castled by hand, protecting the weak b2-pawn.

27...♘c7 28.♖h7 ♕b8 29.♖xf7 ♖xf7 30.♘g1 ♕b3 31.♖d2 ♕a2

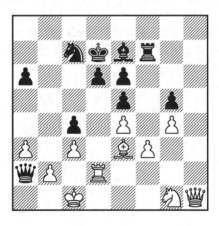

Now the king gets away from the annoying black queen by running to the kingside.

32.♔d1 ♕b3+ 33.♔e2 ♕b8 34.♔f2 ♔c6 35.♔g3

The king has completed the evacuation. With his next move, Black attempts to alter the course of the game by tactical means.

The game now enters the decisive phase. Please observe this knock-down, drag-out battle.

35...d5 36.♕h6 d4!? 37.cxd4 exd4 38.♗xd4 ♘b5+ 39.♔g2 ♘xd4 40.♘e2! ♗f6?

Black had to decide on 40...♘xe2, for example 41.♕xe6+ ♔b5 42.a4+ ♔xa4 43.♕xc4+ ♔a5, when his own king manages to find safe harbor. At the last moment, apparently, Black underestimates his king play. Now everything comes crashing down.

41.♘xd4+ ♔b6 42.♘xe6 ♕e5 43.♕g6

43.♘d8 also works. Now, if Black takes the knight, White has 44.e5.

43...♖e7 44.♘c5

Artistically played. 44.♘f8 or 44.♘d8 also wins.

44...♕f4 45.♖d5 ♔a7 46.e5 ♕e3 47.♕c2 ♖xe5 48.♖d7+ ♔b6 49.♘e4 ♖xe4 50.fxe4 ♗e5 51.♕f2 ♕xf2+ 52.♔xf2 ♗xb2 53.♔e3 1-0

Chapter 8

//

Giving up Castling Voluntarily

Here too, the great Steinitz took the first steps. In the Vienna Game, as well as in the Scotch, he would give up castling voluntarily. Let's try to explain the reason for this policy. In both cases, surrendering castling rights in the game's early stages had a logical basis. Losing the possibility of castling was compensated for, in the first case, by gaining a powerful pawn center; and in the second, by a material advantage. Imagine what kind of furor was stirred up by 5.♔e2!?, especially when tried by one of the world's strongest players – by the very founder of the positional game, with its well worked-out, exact postulates and rules. But here – such novelty! A total turnabout in thinking!

We remind you that it was precisely this idea that inspired Sam Loyd to create the masterpiece we discussed in Chapter 1. True, later games would call into question this particular variation of the Vienna Game (which you may look up at your leisure), but not the idea itself – that is, using the king as an active piece. For an example, look at the Steinitz–Paulsen games.

For the sake of convenience, we advise you to look at the games in the following order (proceeding from Black's move 5) – *5...d6:* Nos. 1, 3, 4, 5; *5...d5:* Nos. 6, 12, 13; *5...b6:* Nos. 2, 8, 9, 10, 11; *5...♕h4+:* No. 7; and *5...♘f6:* No. 14. We give the games in chronological order.

1. W. Steinitz – G. Neumann

Dundee 1867
Vienna Game C25

1.e4 e5 2.♘c3 ♘c6 3.f4 exf4 4.d4 ♕h4+ 5.♔e2

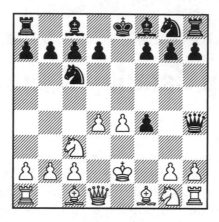

A most original concept by Wilhelm Steinitz!

This was the first among the known games by Steinitz where the idea of voluntarily relinquishing castling came up. In compensation, White gets a powerful pawn center. Interestingly, one of Steinitz's earlier games, where he played Black, also saw this move, but in a somewhat different situation. True, in that game, White was forced into making that move. Who knows – maybe that game played its role in inducing the great Steinitz to take it up?

Here are the first few moves of that almost-unknown game. K. Hamppe – W. Steinitz, Vienna 1859: 1.e4 e5 2.♘c3 ♘f6 3.f4 d5 4.exd5 ♘xd5 5.fxe5 ♘xc3 6.bxc3 ♕h4+ 7.♔e2; and it's not hard to see what a sad situation White has gotten himself into. (Incidentally, *Fritz* evaluates White's position as difficult.)

5...d6 6.♘f3 ♗g4 7.♗xf4 ♗xf3+?!

An unfortunate choice. Practice would later show that it's hard to set White difficult problems this way. It was better to continue development with 7...♘f6 or 7...♘ge7, or to deliver a counterblow to the center with 7...f7-f5!.

8.♔xf3!

The king acts usefully as an ordinary piece, controlling a lot of important squares in the middle of the board. It's interesting that even *Fritz* rates White's position as superior at this point.

8...♘ge7 9.♗e2

9.g3 is more cautious, as after the game move White would have to consider 9...♕f6.

9...0-0-0 10.♗e3 ♕f6+ 11.♔g3 d5 12.♗g4+ ♔b8 13.e5 ♕g6 14.♔f2

14.♕d3 is worth a look.

14...h5

14...f6 or 14...♘f5 are more in the spirit of the position.

15.♗h3

15.♗h3 looks more natural. One must suppose that White intended to meet 15...♘f5 by snapping the knight off, not with 16.♖e1.

15...f6 16.exf6 ♕xf6+ 17.♕f3 ♕xf3+

Either Black overestimates his own chances, or he fails to see that after 17...♕h4+ he could force a draw by repetition.

18.gxf3!

Not only does the pawn protect the king here, but it also takes control of the important squares e4 and g4. In addition, by opening the g-file, White puts Black's backward g-pawn under fire. Now Black needs to tread carefully in order to avoid falling into a bad position. Jumping ahead a little, we can say that Black was unable to deal with this problem. To tell the truth, it must be said that it's not so easy to hold Black's position.

18...g6 19.♘e2 ♘f5

Perhaps he should play 19...♗h6.

20.♗xf5 gxf5 21.c3 ♗d6 22.♗f4 ♔c8 23.♖hg1 ♔d7 24.♖g7+ ♘e7 25.♖ag1 ♔e6? 26.♗xd6

26.♗g5 is simpler.

26...♖xd6

Better 26...♔xd6.

27.♘f4+

27.♘g3 would also set Black great problems.

27...♔f6 28.♘d3

28.h4, fixing Black's pawn on h5, is worth a look.

28...♖b6 29.b3 ♖h6 30.♘e5

Bringing the contest to an end.

30...♖b5 31.a4 ♖a5 32.b4 ♖a6 33.♘d7+ ♔e6 34.♘c5+ 1-0

2. W. Steinitz – J. Minckwitz

Baden-Baden 1870
Vienna Game C25

1.e4 e5 2.♘c3 ♘c6 3.f4 exf4 4.d4 ♕h4+ 5.♔e2 b6

This strong and eminently logical continuation occurs in many of the games in this chapter. Getting ahead of ourselves, we note that White found it difficult to handle the resulting problems.

6.♘b5 ♗a6 7.a4 ♕h5+

7...♘f6 is the more natural move to pose problems for White. Now Steinitz can painlessly finish mobilizing his forces.

8.♘f3 ♝xb5+ 9.axb5 ♕xb5+ 10.♔f2 ♕h5 11.♝xf4 ♘f6 12.e5

12.♝d3 also looks appealing.

12...♘d5

12...♘e4+ is better.

13.♝g3 ♕h6 14.♕e2 ♝e7 15.♕e4 ♕e6 16.♝c4 ♘f6 17.♕e2

17.♕d3 might have been a bit stronger.

17...♘g4+

Black did win because of this move; but 17...♘e4+ is objectively a little stronger.

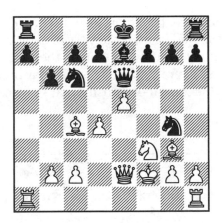

18.♔f1??

When it rains, it pours. 18.♔g1 would maintain the better game for White.

18...♕xc4 0-1

I have to say that the next game is my favorite of the games on the theme of giving up castling, because it fully realizes Steinitz's basic idea. White brilliantly resolves the temporary discomfort of his king's position and then masterfully exploits his lasting advantages – the powerful pawn center and greater space. Black unquestionably played the game passively, but that was because he evidently failed to guess the moves made by the genius Steinitz.

3. W. Steinitz – L. Paulsen

Baden-Baden 1870
Vienna Game C25

1.e4 e5 2.♘c3 ♘c6 3.f4 exf4 4.d4 ♕h4+ 5.♔e2 d6

Along with this move, the alternative 5...b6, as played in the previous game, also looks great. Another interesting line is 5...d5, which will be seen in the remaining games of this chapter.

6.♘f3 ♗g4 7.♗xf4 0-0-0

The principled thrust 7...f5 is worth considering. Kasparov thinks that Black should immediately try to exploit the white king's insecure position; a decent continuation then would appear to be 8.♔d2. In our next game (but not just in that one) Black tries to exploit the white bishop's loose position at f4 by capturing on f3.

8.♔e3!

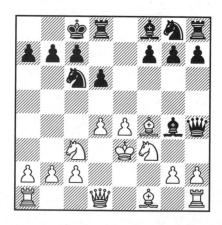

Now the bishop is protected – but at what cost? The king fearlessly protects his army (recall the chapter on the active king). But that's not all!

8...♛h5

And here 8...♝xf3 (Kasparov) is perhaps better suited to the spirit of the position. Any delay helps White: he can cleverly utilize precious time to his benefit. And he did have things to do to make use of the time: along with active operations in the center and on the wings, he could try to tuck the king away in a safe spot.

9.♝e2 ♛a5 10.a3!

This natural move, with a normal idea, involves a very interesting calculation (see White's next move).

10...♝xf3 11.♚xf3!

Both 11.gxf3 g5 12.♝g3 ♝g7 and 11.♝xf3 g5 12.♝g3 ♝g7 promise Black excellent play.

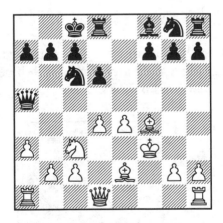

11...♛h5+ 12.♚e3!

How easily does Steinitz reel off the king's moves! Most likely, he did not like the variation 12.♚f2 ♛h4+ 13.g3 ♛f6, although even in this line the advantage lies with White.

12...♕h4 13.b4

White sets about the pawn storm. Black remains without counterplay.

13...g5 14.♗g3 ♕h6 15.b5 ♘ce7 16.♖f1 ♘f6 17.♔f2 ♘g6 18.♔g1

Everybody – come back home!

18...♕g7 19.♕d2 h6 20.a4 ♖g8 21.b6!

This sort of attack has by now become standard, its point being that the attacking side avoids any sort of line-blocking after, say, 21.a5 followed by 22.b6 cxb6 23.axb6 a6.

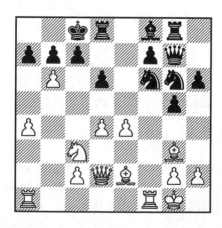

21...axb6

Next comes an elegant concluding combination.

22.♖xf6! ♛xf6 23.♗g4+ ♔b8 24.♘d5 ♛g7 25.a5 f5 26.axb6 cxb6 27.♘xb6 ♘e7 28.exf5 ♛f7 29.f6 ♘c6 30.c4 ♘a7 31.♛a2 ♘b5 32.♘d5 ♛xd5 33.cxd5 ♘xd4 34.♛a7+ ♔c7 35.♖c1+ ♘c6 36.♖xc6# – mate! 1-0

4. W. Steinitz – S. Rosenthal

Baden-Baden 1870
Vienna Game C25

1.e4 e5 2.♘c3 ♘c6 3.f4 exf4 4.d4 ♛h4+ 5.♔e2 d6 6.♘f3 ♗g4 7.♗xf4 ♗xf3+?

An unfortunate choice. A better idea is to continue development with 7...♘f6 or 7...♘ge7.

8.gxf3

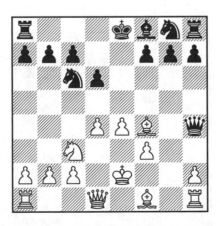

Steinitz's novelty. Apparently, he wished to try out a different continuation (which is also acceptable for White) besides his favorite 8.♔xf3!.

8...♛xf4 9.♘d5 ♛h6?

9...♕h4 is preferable, even though White has a considerable advantage after 10.♘xc7+ ♔d7 11.♘xa8 ♕d8 12.♗h3+ ♔e8. Now Black will not be able to win back the piece on a8.

10.♘xc7+ ♔d8 11.♘xa8 ♔c8 12.d5 ♘f6

Surrender. But things would have fallen apart anyway after 12... ♘e5 13.♕d4 ♔b8 14.♕c3.

The final moves were:

13.dxc6 d5 14.♕d4 ♗d6 15.♕xa7 bxc6 16.♖e1 ♖e8 17.♔d1 dxe4 18.♖xe4 ♖xe4 19.fxe4 ♕f4 20.♗h3+ ♔d8 21.♖f1 ♕xe4 22.♕b6+ ♔e8 23.♖e1 1-0

5. W. Steinitz – J. Minchin/Maj. Martin

Consultation Game, Great Britain 1871
Vienna Game C25

1.e4 e5 2.♘c3 ♘c6 3.f4 exf4 4.d4 ♕h4+ 5.♔e2 d6 6.♘f3 ♗g4 7.♗xf4 ♗f3+?! 8.gxf3 ♘f6 9.♗g3 ♕h5 10.♔f2 0-0-0 11.♗e2

White has a wide range of continuations here: 11.♗c4, 11.♗b5, etc.; but Steinitz apparently planned to follow up with 12.d5 and 13.♕d4. A cursory glance is enough to show that White is on top here.

11...♕a5

Perhaps he should have steeled himself to play 11...d5, meeting 12.e5 with 12...♘g8 13.f4 ♕h6, with an unclear game.

12.d5 ♘e5 13.f4

Here 13.♕d4 gives White an easy game, with the advantage. But Steinitz prefers to enter into complications, where his chances would also be preferable. Our conclusion is: the opening has given White the advantage.

13...♘g6 14.♕d3

14.♕d4 suggests itself; or, to be on the safe side, 14.♔g2.

14...h5 15.h4 ♗e7

One might recommend here the queen check from b6, followed by bringing the knight to g4.

16.b4 ♕b6+

16...♕xb4 might be considered since White cannot continue 17.♖ab1 due to 17...♕xc3.

17.♔f3 ♘g4 18.♖ab1 ♗f6

18...a6 merits attention.

19.a4

(see diagram next page)

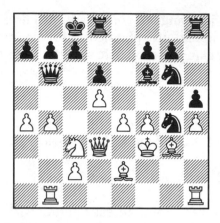

Allows Black a tactical riposte. After 19.♘a4 ♛d4 20.♕xd4 ♝xd4, White stands a little better in the endgame.

19...a6

Black's chances are preferable following 19...♘xf4! 20.♔xf4 ♘f2 21.♕c4 ♝e5+ 22.♔f3 ♘xh1 23.♖xh1 ♝xg3 24.♔xg3 ♕e3+. The sharper variation, winning the queen, is not so clear: 19...♝xc3 20.♕xc3 f5 21.exf5 ♖he8, when after 22.♖b3 ♖e3+ 23.♕xe3 ♘xe3 24.♖xe3 ♘f8 25.c3 we arrive at a most interesting situation where Black is ahead in material but his forces are scattered and his queen is in a danger zone; whereas you can't say the same about the beautifully placed white pieces. On the other hand, serious attention should be paid to 22...♘xf4! instead of winning the queen with 22...♖e3+; this would be most unpleasant for White.

20.♖b3

After 20.a5 ♕a7 21.b5, White could whip up some favorable complications; whereas now Black takes over the initiative and forcibly transposes play into an endgame where he is up in material. If 21...♘xh4+, then 22.♖xh4 (not 22.♝xh4 ♝xh4 23.♘d1 ♘f2!).

20...♘xh4! 21.♖xh4

21.♝xh4? ♝xh4!.

21...♗xh4 22.♔g2 ♗xg3! 23.♕xg3 ♘e3+

23...f5 doesn't look so bad, either.

24.♔h3 h4 25.♕f3 ♘xc2 26.a5 ♕g1 27.♖b1 ♕e3 28.♕xe3 ♘xe3

From this point on, the first world champion demonstrates great defensive skill. Despite his limited forces, with enterprising play he manages to keep setting problems for his opponent.

29.b5! axb5 30.♘xb5 ♖de8 31.♖c1 ♔b8

Black can't play 31...♖xe4?? because of 32.♘xd6+.

32.♗f3 ♖e7

32...f5 is harder for White to meet.

33.a6! bxa6 34.♘d4

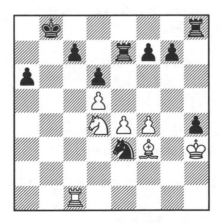

Black's superior forces are somewhat disorganized – which you cannot say about the centralized white pieces, which form a clenched fist, ready to strike. Black needs to play very carefully to make his material advantage count. Experienced chessplayers know how hard it is to find strong moves in the labyrinth of numerous variations – and all the more so when your opponent's pieces come up with their own threats.

34...♔c8 35.♖c3 ♘f1 36.♖b3! g6 37.♘c6

37.♗e2! ♖xe4 38.♗g4+ f5 39.♘xf5 gxf5 40.♗xf5+ ♔d8 41.♗xe4 is worth considering: the definite activity of rook plus bishop, in addition to the small amount of material left on the board, would provide realistic drawing chances.

37...♖ee8 38.e5

38.♗g4+ f5 39.exf5 ♘e3 (39...♖e3+? 40.♖xe3 ♘xe3 41.fxg6+ ♘xg4 42.g7, and White's advanced pawns decide) 40.fxg6+ ♘xg4 41.♔xg4 is more active as White gets some dangerous counterplay.

38...dxe5 39.fxe5 ♘g3

39...♔d7 deserves attention.

40.e6 fxe6 41.dxe6 ♖xe6 42.♖b8+ ♔d7 43.♖xh8 ♖xc6 44.♗xc6+ ♔xc6 45.♔xh4

So Black comes out ahead – but hardly enough to win.

45...♘f5+

45...♘e4 is worth a look; if then 46.♖h6, he might try rapidly pushing the queenside pawns with 46...a5, etc.

46.♔g5 ♘d6 47.♔xg6 ♔b6 48.♔f6 c5 49.♔e6 ♘b7 50.♔d5 ½-½

This game shows, once again, how vigilant both sides have to be in this opening.

6. W. Steinitz – J. Zukertort

London 1872
Vienna Game C25

Steinitz's opponent here, Johannes Zukertort, was one of the world's strongest chessplayers. It was not by accident that in 1886 he played Steinitz in a match to determine the first world champion in chess history. Zukertort was a disciple of Adolf Anderssen – one of the uncrowned world champions and the clearest representative of the Romantic School of chess. It bears noting that, in his youth, Steinitz also belonged to that school; in his later years, however, he abandoned it and became the founder of the Positional School of chess.

But that all came later. For now, let's turn to this game, played in 1872, where we find an aggressive try, the very first attempt at refuting the Steinitz Variation of the Vienna Game with 5...d5.

1.e4 e5 2.♘c3 ♘c6 3.f4 exf4 4.d4 ♕h4+ 5.♔e2 d5!?

An original move, and understandable from a human standpoint. Black seeks to open all the lines of attack as quickly as possible, not eschewing sacrifices. Getting ahead of ourselves a bit, we can say that the great Steinitz was able to demonstrate his understanding of king play at the very highest level. In this situation, the king must execute a most dangerous, yet most entertaining journey in its own defense.

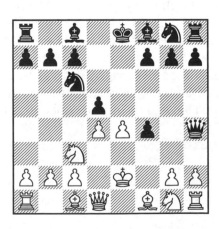

6.exd5

One of the main replies.

6...♗g4+ 7.♘f3 0-0-0

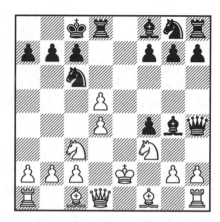

This courageous decision was the result of a man's independent thinking! Soulless *Fritz* shows only the conventional 7...♘ce7, silently condemning the text move. Why does a human choice sometimes fall so completely out of the range of a machine's consideration? We think it's because, for a human being, the game of chess is a struggle; and in the struggle, it's always important to know how to set problems for one's opponent. Meanwhile, for a chess engine, chess is merely the accurate evaluation of all possible continuations. As a result, sometimes the moves a chess engine suggests will generate a storm of protest within us. We like the human move, be it dubious, be it irrational! That human decision to sacrifice a piece for the attack, we cannot compare with a program's. That may be objectively the strongest but, from our point of view, 7...♘ce7 is... stale. We cannot imagine our game without unexpected sacrifices, irrational and non-standard decisions. That's the simplest explanation: we are human!

8.dxc6 ♗c5 9.cxb7+

Only later would players reaching this position start playing 9.♕e1!.

9...♔b8 10.♘b5

A strong move. 10.♕e1 is possible, too.

10...♘f6

Looks natural; but with the brilliant move that follows, Steinitz gets an outstanding position.

11.♔d3!!

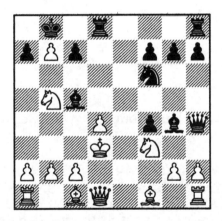

The king is indeed a strong piece – it singlehandedly solves the problem of its own defense!

11...♕h5 12.♔c3

Steinitz believes in his own postulates; still, the prosaic 12.c3 looks better.

12...♗xd4+

Chapter 8

And here it is, the result of that shock that a player feels after unexpected king moves! 12...a6 is necessary here; in that case, White's advantage would not be so overwhelming. Now Steinitz gets a winning position.

13.♘bxd4 ♕c5+ 14.♔b3 ♕b6+ 15.♗b5! ♗xf3 16.♕xf3 ♖xd4 17.♕c6!

Warding off all of the threats.

17...♕a5 18.c3

18.a4! is quite strong here.

18...♖d6 19.♕c4 a6

19...♖b6 deserves a look.

20.♗a4 ♘d5 21.♔a3

A fitting end for the king's journey! White went on to cash in on his material edge:

21...g5 22.b4 ♕b6 23.♕d4 ♕xd4 24.cxd4 ♘b6 25.♗b2 ♘c4+ 26.♔b3 ♘xb2 27.♔xb2 ♖xd4 28.♔c3 ♖hd8 29.♖ad1 ♖4d6 30.♖xd6 ♖xd6 31.♖d1 ♖f6 32.♗c2 ♔xb7 33.♗xh7 ♔b6 34.h3 f3 35.gxf3 ♖xf3+ 36.♖d3 ♖f2 37.a4 a5 38.bxa5+ ♔xa5 39.♖d5+ ♔b6 40.a5+ ♔a7 41.♗d3 ♖f3 42.♖xg5 ♖xh3 43.♖f5 ♖h7 44.♖c5 f5 45.♖xf5 ♖e7 46.♖g5 ♖d7 47.♖e5 ♖g7 48.♖e8 ♖g1 49.♗e4 ♖c1+ 50.♔b4 c5+ 51.♔b5 1-0

A sparkling game!

7. W. Steinitz – J. Dufresne

Liverpool 1874
Vienna Game C25

1.e4 e5 2.♘c3 ♘c6 3.f4 exf4 4.d4 ♕h4+ 5.♔e2 ♕h5+ 6.♘f3 g5

Trying for something different, Black defends the pawn but loses the right to castle. One could not call this plan anything but principled.

7.♘d5 ♔d8 8.♔f2 d6 9.h4! ♗g7

10.c3

A natural, safe move. White now should try to establish communication between his rooks. *Fritz* 12 recommends 10.♗d3. Now the initiative gradually passes over to Black.

10...h6 11.♗d3

11.♔g1, also defending the rook, deserves consideration. If 11...♕g6, then 12.♗d3.

11...♕g6

11...♕g4 leads to a complex position with chances for both sides.

12.hxg5

We might recommend the variation starting with 12.♕c2 proposed by *Fritz*.

12...hxg5 13.♖xh8 ♗xh8 14.g3

This move has an idea behind it. The position has reached the boiling point. Objectively, Black may stand better; but you can see that both sides will have to play very carefully.

14...f5!

A strong move. Black is trying to seize the initiative. After 14... fxg3+ 15.♔xg3 f6, on the other hand, chances are equal.

15.♕h1 ♗g7

15...fxe4 16.♕xh8 exd3 is stronger, with an excellent position for Black.

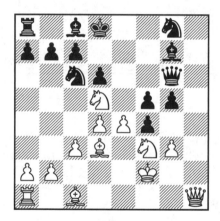

16.♘xg5!

By sharpening the game, Steinitz uses his best practical chance. The struggle now plunges into a maelstrom of complications, which are still easier for White to play thanks to his more active pieces. Black has to play very, very accurately.

16...♕xg5 17.♗xf4 ♕g6 18.♕h4+ ♘ce7

18...♔d7 would run into the brilliant 19.♗g5!. White is a piece down, but his pressure assures him at least an equal game. White's play is clear, while Black has to find "only" moves to avoid falling into a difficult position.

19.♗g5 ♕f7 20.♘xe7 ♘xe7 21.exf5

White has more than sufficient compensation, in the form of a pair of connected passed pawns plus greater activity for all his forces. Steinitz's opponent has been outplayed.

21...♔d7 22.g4 ♘g8 23.♖e1 ♔c6

Played in Steinitz style (the king should resolve its own defensive problems). After the very best move, 23...c6, Black could hope for salvation. For instance, after 24.♕h5 ♕xh5 25.gxh5 ♗f6 26.♖g1 ♔c7 27.h6 ♗xf5! 28.♗xf5 ♗xg5 29.♖xg5 ♘xh6, Black should be able to draw.

Therefore, 24.♗f4 comes into consideration, when Black has problems.

24.d5+!

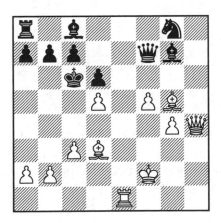

This beautiful, problem-like move puts the final touch to the battle – one not without its mistakes, but rich in content.

24...♔b6 25.♗e3+ c5 26.♕d8+ ♕c7 27.♕xg8 ♗xf5 28.♕xa8 ♗xd3 29.♕e8 ♗e5 30.♗f4 ♗b5 31.♕f8 ♕h7 32.♗xe5 dxe5 33.♕f6+ ♔a5 34.♕xe5 ♕h4+ 35.♔g3 ♕f6+ 36.♔g1 1-0

8. W. Steinitz – W. Parratt

Oxford (blindfold simul) 1875
Vienna Game C25

1.e4 e5 2.♘c3 ♘c6 3.f4 exf4 4.d4 ♕h4+ 5.♔e2 b6!? 6. ♘b5 ♗a6 7.a4 g5

The more energetic 7...♘f6 is worth considering: after 8.♘f3 ♕h6 9.♔e1, the position gets complicated. 7...0-0-0!? is interesting, too.

8.♘f3 ♕h5

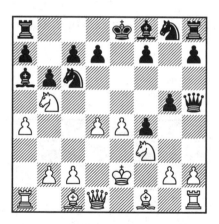

A critical moment – the white king stands at a crossroads. Remember this position, as we will come back to it after we finish the game. Steinitz takes the king away to the queenside. At the same time, he threatens 9.♘xc7+.

9.♔d2 ♔d8

One way or the other, Black had to give up castling. 9...♖c8 looks like the more principled way to do it. The move didn't appeal to Steinitz's opponent since White would still have a discovered attack with ♘xc7 or ♘d6+.

10.c3

Steinitz's favorite move, shoring up his pawn center, looks natural; however, 10.d5 is worth consideration.

10...g4

10...♘f6, as played in Game 9, looks interesting here.

11.♘e1

Here, too, 11.d5 doesn't look bad.

11...♗h6

This looks like a wild shot, whereas simply 11...♘f6 would set White serious problems, e.g. 12.♗d3 d5 13.exd5 ♘xd5 14.♔c2 ♗b7, when White would find it hard to finish developing his queenside.

12.♔c2

Solving the problem of the king's safety. Chances are even for both sides: White has a good pawn center, but he still has to resolve the matter of his development. Black, on the other hand, has easy piece development, while retaining his powerful kingside pawn cluster.

12...♘f6 13.e5 ♘d5

This enables White to strive for the advantage after 14.h3, whereas after 13...♘e4 14.♘d3 ♕f5, the game is even, with Black keeping all of the pluses in his position.

14.♘d3?!

14.♗c4!?.

14...f5

Fritz thinks the strongest move here is 14...♘a5.

15.exf6

Maybe he should pass on the opportunity to capture *en passant*, since now Black's king rook can get into play easily.

15...♘xf6 16.h3 ♕f5?!

Black can't stand the tension. Here 16...♚c8, with the idea of artificial castling and completing development, makes more sense. Now Steinitz, turns things his way with a series of tactical blows.

17.hxg4 ♘xg4

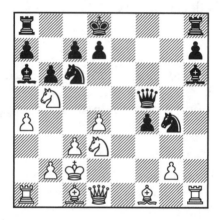

18.♖xh6!

Steinitz is playing the position beautifully. White has the initiative.

18...♘xh6 19.♗xf4

Double attack.

19...♘f7 20.♕f3!

20.♘xc7 looks tempting, but Steinitz's sharp eye caught the counterstroke 20...♘xd4+!, when after a tactical back-and-forth, Black would maintain the balance with strong counterplay. For example: 21.♚b1 (21.cxd4? is bad in light of 21...♖c8, when Black is on top) 21...♗xd3+ 22.♗xd3 ♕xf4 23.♘xa8 ♘e6 (23...♘c6 doesn't look bad, either), and if 24.a5 here, then 24...♚e7.

20...♚c8?

20...♕g6 is necessary. Now White gets a great advantage.

21.♘xc7 ♗b7 22.♕g3 ♕g6 23.♘xa8 ♗xa8 24.♖e1

He might also have played 24.♕xg6 hxg6 25.♖e1, leaving him with a healthy extra pawn, the two bishops, and every chance of winning.

24...♕xg3 25.♗xg3 ♘cd8 26.♗h4 h6 27.♖e7

27.♘f4 wins easily.

27...♘d6 28.♘f4

28.g4, protecting the f5 square, suggests itself.

28...♘8f7

It's strange that Black didn't try the natural 28...♘f5, after which he might have been able to draw: 29.♘g6 ♖g8 30.♗d3 ♘xh4 31.♘xh4 ♖g4.

29.♗d3 ♗b7 30.g4 ♗f3 31.♘g6 ♖e8 32.♖xe8+ ♘xe8

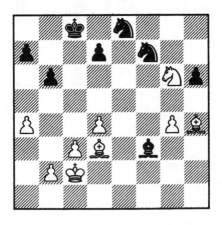

In this winning position, Steinitz unexpectedly agreed to a draw. The fact that he was playing several games blindfolded at the same time may have had something to do with this.

½-½

This game showed that a massive pawn cluster on the kingside, in combination with active pieces, could be a strong argument for Black against White's powerful pawn center. Were it not for Black's error on move 16, White would have had to mount a difficult defense; it would have been hard to advise White on how to bring out his queenside pieces – look at the sad fate of the c1-bishop. Remember that Steinitz would justify the temporary disruption caused by the loss of his right to castle, by pointing to White's powerful pawn center. But, as we have just seen in this game, White's center is his only compensation for Black's indisputable advantage. Can we say that this whole variation has been put under a cloud? I believe it is too soon to tell. Let's return to the position after Black's move 8:

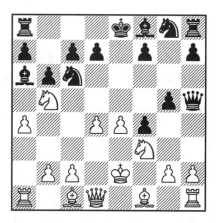

White needs to decide what to do with his king. Remember: after 9.♔f2, there comes 9...♗xb5 10.axb5 ♘xd4!.

This is what happened in Steinitz – D. Martínez, match II (1), Philadelphia 1882. The game continued 11.c3 ♘xf3 12.gxf3 ♗c5+ 13.♔e2. Here Black could have gotten an excellent position with

13...♘e7. But after 13...♘f6 – a much less fortunate move – the position grew quite sharp, with mutual chances; and in the end, this entertaining battle came out in Martínez's favor.

On the other hand the natural move, 9.♔d2, as played by our first world champion, led to a difficult game. But, what if the queen were to defend from a different square (9.♔e1)? The threat of capturing on c7 would force Black into 9...♖c8, 9...♔d8, or 9...♗xb5. In all cases, White's position would come out at least a little better.

But the most interesting thing in all this, is that this typically Steinitzian move was also the one suggested by *Fritz!*

Here is the game we were just talking about.

9. W. Steinitz – D. Martínez

Match II (1), Philadelphia 1882
Vienna Game C25

1.e4 e5 2.♘c3 ♘c6 3.f4 exf4 4.d4 ♕h4+ 5.♔e2 b6 6.♘b5 ♗a6 7.a4 g5 8.♘f3 ♕h5 9.♔f2?? ♗xb5 10.axb5

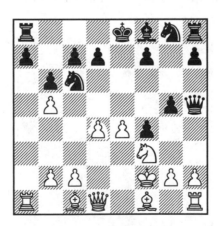

10...♘xd4! 11.c3 ♘xf3 12.gxf3 ♗c5+ 13.♔e2 ♘f6

As we said, 13...♘e7 is stronger.

14.e5 ♘g8 15.b4 ♗f8 16.♕d4 ♗g7 17.♕e4 ♖c8 18.h4 ♕g6
19.hxg5 ♕xe4+ 20.fxe4 ♗xe5 21.♖xa7 ♘e7 22.c4 ♘g6
23.♗h3 ♘f8 24.♖d1 ♘e6 25.c5 d6 26.♖b7 ♖g8 27.♗xe6
fxe6 28.♖h1 dxc5 29.bxc5 bxc5 30.♖xh7 ♖xg5 31.b6 ♖g2+
32.♔f3 ♖g3+ 33.♔e2 ♖b3 34.♖h5 f3+ 35.♔d1 ♖d8+ 36.♔c2
♖c3+ 37.♔b1 ♖xc1+ 38.♔xc1 f2 39.♖h1 cxb6 40.♖xb6 ♔f7
41.♖f1 ♗d4 42.♔d2 ♔f6 43.♔e2 ♖g8 44.♔f3 ♔e5 45.♖c6
♖f8+ 46.♔e2 ♖f4 47.♔d3 ♖f3+ 48.♔e2 ♖h3 49.♔d2 ♖h4
50.♔d3 ♖f4 51.♖a6 ♖f3+ 52.♔d2 ♖f6 53.♔d3 ♔f4 54.♖a2
♔f3 55.e5 ♖f5 56.♖e2 c4+ 57.♔d2 c3+ 58.♔d1 ♔g2 0-1

Even in this losing cause, Steinitz battled like a true fighter!

10. W. Steinitz – D. Martínez

Match II (3), Philadelphia 1882
Vienna Game C25

1.e4 e5 2.♘c3 ♘c6 3.f4 exf4 4.d4 ♕h4+ 5.♔e2 b6 6.♘b5
♗a6 7.a4 g5 8.♘f3 ♕h5 9.♔d2 ♔d8 10.c3 ♘f6 11.♗d3 ♘g4

Better is 11...g4, driving the knight back as in Steinitz–Parratt
above, with advantage to Black. It looks like White's in a bad way...

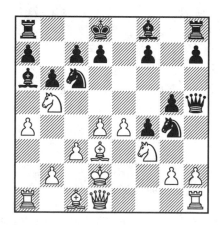

...but now comes the Steinitzian

12.♔e2!!

and the two sides' chances are once again equal.

12...♘e3 13.♗xe3 fxe3 14.♔xe3

Seeing this move is getting to be a habit.

14...g4 15.♘d2

In the next game between the same two players, we will see 15.♘e1.

15...♕g5+ 16.♔e2

16.♔f2!?.

16...♗h6 17.♘f1

Passive: 17.♘c4 is better.

17...d5

Played in the spirit of the position, but 17...f5!? might have given White more complicated problems to solve.

18.exd5 g3?

An oversight. An alternative is 18...♘b4, when Black wins after 19.cxb4 ♖e8+ 20.♔f2 ♕f4+ 21.♔g1 ♗xb5 22.♗xb5 ♗g7!.

19.hxg3 ♕f6 20.♖xh6

This is what Black missed.

Now White gets a practically winning position, although 20.♘d2 is also possible here.

20...♖e8+ 21.♔d2 ♕xh6+ 22.♔c2 ♘e7 23.♕f3 ♗b7 24.c4 a6 25.♘c3 ♕g7 26.♕f2 ♔d7 27.♘e4

The simple 27.♘d2 looks good, too.

27...f5 28.♘ed2 ♖f8 29.♘f3 ♖ae8 30.♘e3 ♚d8 31.♘e5 ♛g5 32.♛f4! ♛h5 33.a5! b5 34.cxb5 ♘xd5 35.♘xd5 ♗xd5 36.bxa6 ♚c8 37.♖c1 h6 38.♚b1 ♛g5 39.♛f1 ♛f6 40.♛e1

40.♖c5 is more active.

40...♛d6 41.♛f2 ♚b8 42.♛d2 ♚a8 43.♛c2 ♖e7

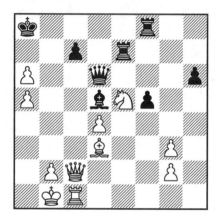

44.♗c4??

An unfortunate mistake in a winning position.

44...♗e4 45.♗d3

And here, 45.♘d3 is better. Now it is Black who has the upper hand.

45...♖xe5 46.dxe5 ♛xd3 47.♛xd3 ♗xd3+ 48.♚a2

The balance has swung in Black's favor – and yet, the game still ends in a draw. Of course, Black didn't make the most of his resources.

48...♗b8 49.♖c6 ♖e8 50.a7+ ♔b7 51.♖c5 ♗e4 52.♔b3 c6 53.♔c3 h5 54.♔d4 ♔xa7 55.b4 ♔a6 56.♔e3 ♖e6 57.g4 hxg4 58.g3 ♔b7 59.♔f4 ♗b1 60.♔g5 ♗d3 61.♖c3 ♗e4 62.♖c5 ♔b8 63.♔f4 ♖g6 64.♖c4 ♖e6 65.♖d4 ♔c7 66.♖c4 ♔d7 67.♖d4+ ♔e7 68.♖d1 ♖g6 69.♖a1 ♖g8 70.a6 ♖a8 71.a7 ♔e6 72.♖a5 ♗d3 73.♖a3 ♗c4 74.♖a1 ♗d3 ½-½

The opening phase of this game was much the same as in Steinitz's game with Parratt; our conclusion is the same as it was for that game: thanks to his well-developed pieces and powerful kingside pawn cluster, Black can count on a comfortable game. On the other hand White, despite his pawn center, will have to spend a great deal of time solving the problem of developing several of his pieces, should Black play 11...g4.

11. W. Steinitz – D. Martínez

Match II (7), Philadelphia 1882
Vienna Game C25

1.e4 e5 2.♘c3 ♘c6 3.f4 exf4 4.d4 ♕h4+ 5.♔e2 b6 6.♘b5 ♗a6 7.a4 g5 8.♘f3 ♕h5 9.♔d2

Black failed to resolve his opening problems in Game 7 of the first match between these two opponents: 9...♗xb5 10.axb5 ♘a5 11.c3 ♘f6 12.♗d3 ♘g4?! (12...g4!?) 13.♘e5! ♘f6 14.♕xh5 ♘xh5 15.♔c2 f6 16.♘f3 c5? 17.dxc5 ♖c8 18.b4 ♘b7 19.♖xa7, and White won easily.

9...♔d8 10.c3 ♘f6 11.♗d3 ♘g4 12.♔e2 ♘e3 13.♗xe3 fxe3 14.♔xe3 g4 15.♘e1

In the previous game, Steinitz had retreated his king to d2.

15...♗h6+ 16.♔f2 ♕g5 17.g3

We can only assume that Steinitz did not like 17.♘c2 because of 17...♖g8. But now Black tries a pawn break in the center to open up the game.

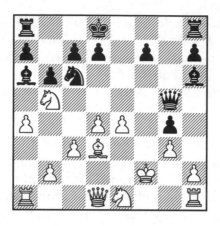

17...f5?! 18.exf5

Challenge accepted! Again, getting ahead of ourselves a bit, we note that this first world champion made a habit of throwing himself into complications. On move 17, ...♗b7 is worth considering.

18...♘e7 19.♘g2 ♘xf5 20.♖e1! ♖f8 21.♔g1

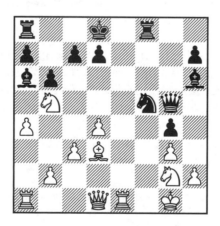

Just as in his brilliant game against Paulsen, Steinitz has succeeded in resolving his temporary issues. You've got to love the king's journey: ♔e1-e2-d2-e2xe3-f2-g1. But here, unlike in the aforementioned game, the play had an even character, because White lacks the advantage of a strong pawn center. Even though White eventually scored the point, we believe that Steinitz's original idea gave him no advantage, either out of the opening or in the early middlegame.

21...♗b7 22.♗e4 ♗xe4 23.♖xe4 a6

The normal 23...c6, with artificial castling to follow, guarantees Black an easy game.

24.♘a3 ♖g8 25.♕b3

25.♘c4 is stronger; if 25...d5?, then he can play for a fork with 26.♘f4! or 26.♘e5.

25...♕g6 26.♖f1 ♘d6 27.♖e5 ♖f8 28.♖xf8+ ♗xf8 29.♕d1

29.♘f4 looks more energetic. It's interesting that the black queen has no invasion squares, and must therefore retreat.

29...♔c8 30.♘f4 ♕g8

From this point on, the game seems to have proceeded in mutual time pressure, as reflected in the quality of the moves.

31.♘d5 ♔b7 32.♘e3 ♘f7 33.♖e4 h5 34.♘ac4 d5 35.♘a5+ bxa5 36.♕b3+ ♔a7 37.♕xd5 ♕g6 38.♖f4 ♗h6 39.♕c5+ ♕b6 40.♕xb6+ ♔xb6 41.♖f6+ ♔b7 42.♘f5 ♗c1 43.♖xf7 ♗xb2 44.c4 ♖d8 45.d5 ♗a3 46.♔f2 ♔b6 47.♔e2 ♖e8+ 48.♔d3 ♖e1 49.♖f6+ ♔b7 50.♖e6 ♖d1+ 51.♔c2 ♖f1 52.♘d4 ♖f2+ 53.♖e2 ♖xe2+ 54.♘xe2 ♗e7 55.♘c3 c6 56.♘e4 cxd5 57.cxd5 h4 58.♔d3 hxg3 59.hxg3 ♔c7 60.♔e3 ♗d6 61.♘xd6 ♔xd6 62.♔f4 ♔xd5 63.♔xg4 ♔c4 64.♔f5 ♔b4 65.g4 ♔xa4 66.g5 ♔b5 67.g6 a4 68.g7 a3 69.g8♕ 1-0

12. W. Steinitz – M. Chigorin

London 1883
Vienna Game C25

Steinitz's opponent in this game was the Russian champion, Mikhail Chigorin, who played two matches with Steinitz for the world championship. Chigorin was a follower of the Romantic School. Only Steinitz was able to block his path to the world title. Chigorin has many of the most interesting, substantial games to his credit; we believe that young players would greatly benefit from examining the games of this remarkable chessplayer.

1.e4 e5 2.♘c3 ♘c6 3.f4 exf4 4.d4 ♕h4+ 5.♔e2 d5

We already saw this move in Game 6 above.

6.exd5 ♕e7+

A new twist. This way, Mikhail Chigorin tries to show that Black can either make a draw or force White to take a big risk in order to avoid the draw. In Game 6, Zukertort played 6...♗g4+.

7.♔f2 ♕h4+ 8.g3!

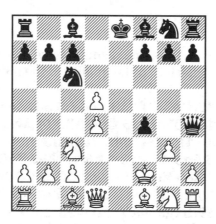

The exclamation point is for courage, although this move is strong in and of itself. The first world champion was not a timid fellow. And so, the challenge is accepted. Now the game enters a phase of unbelievable complexity.

8...fxg3+ 9.♔g2 ♗d6

9...♘xd4!?.

10.♕e1+! ♘ce7

10...♕e7 would have led to head-spinning complications, e.g. 11.♗g5 f6 12.♕d2.

11.hxg3 ♕xd4 12.♖h4

12.♘f3 is worth a serious look: there could follow 12...♕g4 13.♖h4 ♕g6 14.♗b5+ or 14.♗d3 with the better chances. Now the position evens out.

12...♕f6 13.♘e4

Quite logical, although 13.♘f3 is interesting.

13...♕g6 14.♗d3 ♗f5 15.♘xd6+

This looks both natural and strong. But subsequent developments in the battle show that Black's position is completely defensible, and then some. In the interval between moves 12 and 16, Steinitz was determined to show the insubstantiality of Black's chosen defense, leading to the sad outcome of this game. Simply 15.♘f3 guarantees equality.

15...cxd6 16.♗b5+ ♔f8 17.c4 ♘f6

By now, one might prefer Chigorin's position.

18.♘f3 ♗g4

18...♗e4 looks very, very strong here. Now White gets to confuse matters with enterprising play.

19.♘d4 ♘f5 20.♘xf5 ♕xf5 21.♗f4 g5

21...h5!.

22.♗xd6+ ♔g7

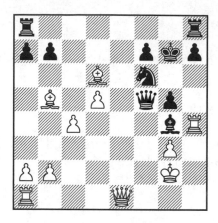

23.⧸xg4!

There's Steinitz for you! Vigorous play has allowed him to reach an unclear position. The bishop pair, his powerful pawn cluster in the center, and the somewhat insecure position of Black's king – together, all of these amount to compensation for the material deficit. We think that, now, most players would prefer to have White, as his plan of play is clearer.

23...♘xg4 24.♕c3+

It's hard to see how this natural move could be the decisive error. After the strongest move, 24.♕e2, there's a whole long struggle ahead.

24...f6

Unexpectedly, now the unfortunate placement of White's king is the telling factor. Chigorin confidently carries the battle to victory.

25.♖f1 ♕e4+ 26.♔g1 ♕e2 27.♖f3 ♖he8 28.♗xe8 ♖xe8

All of the black pieces participate in the attack – which cannot be said of the white ones.

29.♗c5 ♕h2+ 30.♔f1 ♖e2 0-1

13. W. Steinitz – J. Zukertort

World Chp (20), New Orleans/New York 1886
Vienna Game C25

This turned out to be the final game of the first match in history
to decide the chess championship of the world.

**1.e4 e5 2.♘c3 ♘c6 3.f4 exf4 4.d4 d5 5.exd5 ♕h4+ 6.♔e2
♕e7+ 7.♔f2**

7.♔f3 seems riskier to us: after 7...♕h4 8.♔e2 ♕e7+ 9.♔f3, the
game Steinitz–J. Mackenzie, New York 1883, ended in a draw. I
should mention one little interesting detail: we have grown ac-
customed to the first world champion's risky playing style, so we
should not be surprised by White's move 7. After 7...♘f6, the game
could have entered into tactical complexities, with Black enjoying
somewhat the better chances (we remain certain that Steinitz well
understood this); but Steinitz would willingly jump into the fire, giving his opponent a kind of odds – and his opponent refused. Therefore, in this short little game, Steinitz was the psychological winner.

7...♕h4+ 8.g3 fxg3 9.♔g2 ♘xd4

In this position we already know about Chigorin's 9...♗d6. The
text move is strong, but it requires more accurate play from Black:
he has to balance on a knife's edge, although objectively speaking
his position is quite defensible (especially if you possess a powerful
chess engine!).

10.hxg3

The normal reaction. Steinitz correctly thinks that 10.♕e1+ leads
to unclear play.

10...♕g4 11.♕e1+

He should have developed a piece – say, his dark-squared bishop.

11...♗e7 12.♗d3! ♘f5

A tragic mistake, leading to defeat. In his analysis, Steinitz notes that, given his threat to move the rook to h4, the black king should get out of the pin with 12...♔d8. *Fritz*, however, correctly suggests another Steinitzian move: 12...♔f8, with very complicated play.

13.♘f3

Simplest. Other winning moves are also possible.

13...♗d7 14.♗f4

We suspect that Steinitz rejected 14.♘e5 due to the original counterstroke 14...♕xg3+.

14...f6 15.♘e4! ♘gh6

Allows the winning combination. Truth be told, however, Black no longer has a defense.

16.♗xh6 ♘xh6

17.♖xh6 gxh6 18.♘xf6+ ♔f7 19.♘xg4 1-0

14. M. Chigorin – W. Steinitz

World Chp (21), La Habana 1892
Vienna Game C25

This game is doubly interesting, in that this time it was Steinitz's opponent, Chigorin, who played the Vienna as White. And in a world championship match, no less!

1.e4 e5 2.♘c3 ♘c6 3.f4 exf4 4.d4 ♕h4+ 5.♔e2 ♘f6

Steinitz chooses a solid move.

6.♘f3 ♕g4 7.d5!?

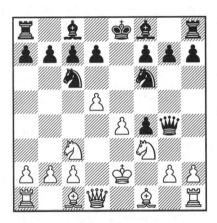

As always, Mikhail Chigorin chooses the active path, immediately setting Black a problem. It's interesting: was Steinitz prepared for this turn of events?

7...♘e5

The computer's variation, 7...♘b4 8.a3 ♘a6 9.e5 ♘h5 10.b4, leads to unclear play.

8.h3 ♕h5 9.♗xf4 ♘xf3

From a tactical viewpoint, 9...♗d6!? looks original. Now White gets a solid advantage.

10.gxf3 d6

Playing it safe and solid. But maybe he should have ignored the threat and played 10...♗c5, and if 11.♗xc7, then 11...d6. Experience teaches us that Black would have sufficient compensation. Or if 11.e5, then 11...♕f5 ensures a normal game for him.

11.♔d2

11.♘b5 is worth considering, as Black would have to forfeit castling with 11...♔d8.

11...♕h4

Steinitz is true to himself. Now he goes in for complications, which raises the importance of each move. This fierce style of play was something he often employed in this variation – but on White's side! An alternative is 11...♗d7, controlling the b5 square.

12.♗e3 ♗e7 13.♘b5 ♗d8 14.♘xa7 ♗d7 15.♘b5

White wins a pawn. However, this comes at the cost of valuable time, and of the advantage to boot.

The active 15.♗b5 would have been met by 15...♖xa7 16.♗xd7+ ♘xd7 17.♗xa7 b6, with unclear play. Is it possible that going after that pawn was not worth the time invested?

15...0-0 16.♘c3

(see diagram next page)

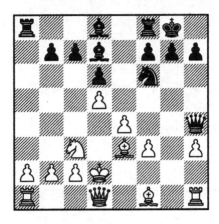

16...♘h5! 17.♕e1 ♘g3 18.♖g1 ♘xf1+ 19.♕xf1 f5!

Black has taken the initiative with his vigorous play. White gradually drifts into a hopeless position.

20.♕g2 ♖f7 21.♖h1 ♗f6! 22.♘d1 ♖e8

22...fxe4 also looks great.

23.f4 ♖xe4

Enough to win, although 23...fxe4 deserves attention.

24.c3 ♖fe7 25.♖e1 ♖xf4

Black is winning.

26.♗f2 ♕h5 27.♗e3 ♕h4 28.♗f2 ♕g5 29.♕xg5 ♗xg5 30.♗e3 ♖fe4

30...♗h4 is more muscular.

31.♗xg5 ♖xe1 32.♗xe7 ♖xe7

White now has only some practical chances to survive.

33.♘f2 ♚f7

Black here could play 33...♝b5 with tempo.

34.c4 g5 35.a4 f4 36.a5 ♝c8

36...h5 is simpler.

37.b4 f3 38.♖e1 ♖xe1 39.♚xe1 h5 40.♚d2 g4 41.h4 ♝f5

Apparently, Black had hoped to win quickly after 41...g3. But then White would have had a hidden tactical resource with 42.♘e4!, when if 42...g2, then 43.♘g5+ with practical chances for salvation – although, in this case, the first player still would have to follow a tortuous path to safety.

42.♘h1 ♚e7 43.♘g3 ♝g6 44.♚e3 ♚d7 45.b5 ♚c8 46.♚d4 ♚b8 47.♚e3 ½-½

A draw was agreed here, even though all the resources are not yet exhausted. On the principled move 47...c6, there might follow 48.bxc6 bxc6 49.c5!!, with a probable draw.

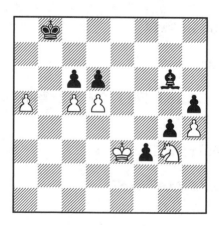

An engrossing battle between two chess geniuses!

15. J.H. Blackburne – W. Steinitz

Match (2), London 1876
Scotch Game C45

And now we bring to the reader's attention Steinitz's favorite variation in the Scotch Game. The basic idea in this line is that Black voluntarily gives up castling, sheltering his king behind a wall of pawns, capped by the d6-pawn. This is how Steinitz would throw down the gauntlet to his opponents: from the very first moves, he would draw them into hand-to-hand combat. Black wins a center pawn, but White gets the opportunity to launch an attack against the black king, which is stranded in the center. The defending side, naturally, follows a strategy of simplification. Black usually prevails if he manages to trade off the queens. In a word: right out of the opening – just as in the Steinitz Gambit of the Vienna Game – we have an engrossing and uncompromising fight.

In the three games that follow, Steinitz's opponent was Joseph Henry Blackburne, an outstanding English player of the nineteenth century who in 1892 would challenge the then-reigning world champion, Emanuel Lasker.

1.e4 e5 2.♘f3 ♘c6 3.d4 exd4 4.♘xd4 ♕h4!?

Already on move 5, White must decide how to defend his e-pawn.

5.♘b5

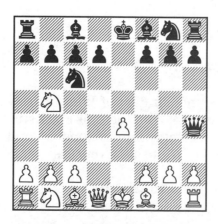

White selects the most aggressive continuation. 5.♘c3 is also quite possible, to which 5...♝b4 is considered the best reply.

5...♝b4+

The active 5...♝c5 also looks good.

5...♕xe4+ occurred in Paulsen–Steinitz, Vienna 1882: 6.♝e3 ♕e5 7.♘d2 ♚d8 8.c3 ♝c5 9.♘c4 ♕e7 10.♝e2 ♝xe3 11.♘xe3 ♘f6 12.0-0 d6 13.c4 a6 14.♘c3 ♕e5 15.♖e1 ♖e8 16.♖c1 ♘d4 17.b4 a5 18.b5 c5 19.bxc6 bxc6 20.h3 ♝d7, with a complex battle and equal chances in a game ultimately won by Steinitz.

6.♝d2 ♕xe4+ 7.♝e2 ♚d8

A natural move, for Steinitz. The king acts like a regular piece, defending a pawn.

8.0-0 ♝xd2 9.♕xd2 ♘f6

In later games, Steinitz would opt for the safer 9...a6. Now Black comes under a very strong attack.

10.♘1c3 ♕e5 11.♖fe1 a6 12.♘a3

After 12.♝f3, Black would have a hard time finding good moves.

12...♕d4

12...♕c5 looks more cautious to us.

13.♕g5 ♖g8 14.♖ad1

Completing the mobilization of White's army. We would undoubtedly prefer to have White here, as Black still has not resolved his basic problems: completing development and getting his king to safety. Meanwhile, White has a very easy game.

14...h6 15.♕g3 ♕e5 16.♕h4 ♕g5

We can understand Black's efforts to trade; but *Fritz*'s suggestion, 16...♖e8, looks quite attractive. This is a move that could fall outside the attention of anybody, even of players of the highest caliber.

17.♕c4 ♘e5

Alternatively, Black can play 17...♖f8.

18.♕b4 ♘c6 19.♕b3 ♖f8 20.♘c4

Also possible are 20.♗f3 or 20.♘d5 – in each case, White has good play. The move chosen by Blackburne is not bad, either.

20...b5 21.♗f3! ♗b7

21...bxc4 meets with 22.♕a3.

22.♘d5

A dangerous situation has arisen. The white pieces have taken up menacing posts. One false move from Black and his position will collapse like a house of cards. Worthy of attention is 22.♘d2.

22...♖b8

22...♚c8, threatening to take on c4 and taking the king further away from the danger zone, deserves consideration. Now Black's position becomes rather dubious.

23.♕a3 ♖g8 24.♘e5

White wins easily with either 24.♘d6! or 24.♘xf6!. The text move also leads to victory.

24...♘xe5 25.♕e7+ ♚c8 26.♖xe5 ♘xd5 27.♕xf7 ♕d8 28.♗xd5 ♗xd5 29.♖exd5 d6 30.♖5d3

I don't understand this tiptoeing about: it's time for something brutal! Like 30.♕e6+ ♚b7 31.♖xd6 cxd6 32.♖xd6, promising White a winning position. Probably time pressure...

30...♕e8! 31.♕d5 ♖f8 32.♕d4 ♖f6 33.♖e3 ♕c6 34.♖de1 ♚b7

Black has consolidated his position, nearly equalizing.

35.♖c3 ♕d7

35...♖e8 is stronger.

36.♖ce3 ♖bf8 37.f3 ♖8f7 38.♖e8 ♕c6 39.c3 ♖f5 40.♖8e7?

Rudderless play by White leads to this mistake.

40...♖d5

Now the initiative passes over to Black, and he briskly realizes his advantage. It is possible that White didn't make full use of his saving chances; but we are fully aware of how difficult it can be, during a game, to shift gears to a stubborn defense when we had enjoyed a winning position just a short while before.

41.♕h4 ♕c5+ 42.♚f1 g5 43.♕e4 ♖xe7 44.♕xe7 ♖d2 45.♖e2 ♖d1+ 46.♖e1 ♕c4+ 47.♕e2 ♖xe1+ 48.♚xe1 ♕xa2 49.♕e4+

d5 50.♕c2 ♕c4 51.♕d2 a5 52.g3 b4 53.f4 gxf4 54.gxf4 bxc3 55.bxc3 a4 56.♔d1 a3 57.♔c1 ♔c6 58.♔b1 ♕b3+ 59.♔a1 ♔d6 60.♕c1 ♔e7 61.♕d2 ♔f7 62.♕c1 c5 63.♕d2 ♔f6 64.♕c1 ♔f5 65.♕d2 ♕b2+ 66.♕xb2 axb2+ 67.♔xb2 ♔xf4 0-1

And so, Black won – yet he had stood to lose. We present these kinds of games with the express purpose of highlighting the difficulties that Black may face in this variation. In our next game, Steinitz adjusted his opening play.

16. J.H. Blackburne – W. Steinitz

Match (4), London 1876
Scotch Game C45

1.e4 e5 2.♘f3 ♘c6 3.d4 exd4 4.♘xd4 ♕h4 5.♘b5 ♗b4+ 6.♗d2 ♕xe4+ 7.♗e2 ♔d8 8.0-0 ♗xd2 9.♕xd2 a6

An improvement over the previous game. Steinitz rightly decides to attack the knight at once.

10.♘1c3 ♕e5

10...♕h4 is safer. Steinitz utilized this square for the queen in the sixth match game against Golmayo in 1883 (see Game 19). True, in that game the queen was attacked by the knight moving from b5 to c3.

11.♘a3 b5?!

11...♕d4! looks both better and safer. But we know about Steinitz's fighting character, don't we? How often does he lure his opponent into going with him to the brink of disaster! Let's see how this turns out here.

12.♗f3 ♘ge7 13.♖ad1 ♕f5

The variation 13...b4 14.♘d5 bxa3 15.♘xe7 ♕xe7 16.♗xc6 ♖b8 17.♗xd7 ♗xd7 18.♖fe1 ♕d6 19.♕g5+ ♕f6 20.♕g4 shows us the kind of incredibly complex problems Black faced. One careless step could spoil the whole game for him.

14.罩fe1 罩b8

14...罩e8 might be better.

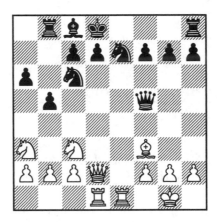

A critical position: White's piece activity has reached its zenith. In such situations, a quality player will often look for a combination or a forcing maneuver leading to a decisive attack. But we also know that getting lost in the labyrinthine multitude of variations can lead to the loss of a significant amount of one's advantage. How many games have been spoiled this way! This game is an example of it. In the critical position, White fails to follow the best course. We've already said how useful detailed analysis is: afterward, we can verify our variations with a chess engine. But do not lose hope under any circumstances, even if your engine doesn't rate your ideas very highly. Very often, it will change its preliminary assessments in favor of human ones.

15.營e2

Rather lifeless. Please analyze the following lines:

a) 15.皇e4! 營f6 16.皇xc6 公xc6 17.公d5 營h6; or

b) 15.皇xc6!? 公xc6 16.公d5 皇b7 (16...d6 17.營c3) 17.營c3 罩g8 18.b4 (18.營g3 d6).

15...d6

Now Black consolidates his position and the worst is over for him.

16.♘e4 ♗d7

16...♗e6!.

17.♕e3 f6 18.g4

In a slightly better position, Blackburne burns his bridges.

18...♕g6 19.♘xd6

19...cxd6 20.♖xd6 ♔c7

20...♘e5 looks more forceful. After that move, it would be hard to tell White how to continue the attack.

21.♗xc6

We have to think that White overlooked Black's move 22, else he would have played 21.♕c5 to continue the struggle. Even so, Black would enjoy excellent play after 21...♕g5. We should also mention that here the combination with 22.♖xe7 leads to a difficult ending after 22...♕xc5 23.♖exd7+ ♔b6 24.♖xc6+ ♕xc6 25.♗xc6 ♔xc6.

21...♞xc6 22.♕g3 ♚c8! 23.♖ed1 ♖b7 24.♕g2 ♞b8! 25.♖1d4 h5 26.♕d5 ♕g5

That's it – game over. The game concluded:

27.♕xg5 fxg5 28.♖g6 ♝xg4 29.♖xg5 ♖e8 30.♚g2 ♖f7 31.h3 ♝d7 32.♚g3 ♖e2 33.♖xh5 ♖exf2 34.♖c5+ ♞c6 35.♖d3 ♚c7 36.♞b1 ♚b6 37.♖cd5 ♞b8 38.♞d2 ♝c6 39.♞e4 ♖e2 40.♞c3 ♖xc2 41.♖d2 ♖xc3+ 42.bxc3 ♝xd5 43.♖xd5 ♖c7 44.♖d3 ♞c6 45.♚f4 ♖f7+ 46.♚e4 ♖f2 47.a3 ♖a2 48.c4 bxc4 49.♖g3 ♖d2 50.♖xg7 ♖d4+ 51.♚f5 c3 0-1

17. J.H. Blackburne – W. Steinitz

Match (6), London 1876
Scotch Game C45

1.e4 e5 2.♞f3 ♞c6 3.d4 exd4 4.♞xd4 ♕h4 5.♞b5 ♝b4+ 6.♝d2 ♕xe4+ 7.♝e2 ♚d8 8.0-0 ♝xd2 9.♕xd2

The knight recapture with 9.♞xd2 doesn't look bad, either.

9...a6 10.♞5a3?!

10.♞1c3!.

10...♕d4!

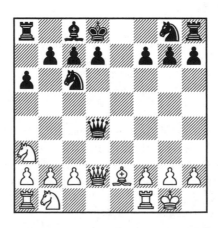

Clearly the strongest continuation, setting White serious problems.

11.♕g5+

11.♕c1 is worth considering.

11...♕f6 12.♕d2

Somewhat risky. Once again, 12.♕c1 is better, or else he could retreat to g3.

12...♕xb2 13.♘c4

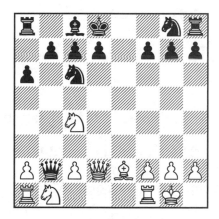

13...♕d4 14.♕c1

Also possible is 14.♗d3.

14...♘ge7

Once again, Black decides against trading the queen for two rooks with 14...♕xa1 15.♕a3! ♘f6 16.♘c3 ♕xf1+ 17.♔xf1, although in that case his advantage would be beyond dispute.

15.♘bd2 d6

All according to plan: Black's pawn phalanx defends his king against any frontal attack on the d-file. More energetic is 15...d5 16.♘e3 ♗e6, with a tremendous game.

16.♖d1 ♗e6 17.♕a3 ♘d5 18.♘b3 ♕c3 19.♗f1

The sharper 19.♘xd6 promises nothing good, e.g. 19...cxd6 20.♕xd6+ ♔c8 21.♖xd5 ♗xd5 22.♕xd5 ♖e8.

19...♘db4 20.♘e3 ♖e8 21.♖d2 ♗xb3

Worthy of attention is the typical Steinitzian evacuation with 21...♔e7.

22.♖ad1 ♖xe3 23.fxe3 ♘xc2

Black is winning.

24.♕c1

Even the superior 24.♕xb3 fails to bring salvation.

24...♕xe3+ 25.♔h1 ♗a4 26.♗c4 ♘2d4

He might have considered the solid 26...f6.

27.♖e1 ♕f4 28.♖f1 ♕h6 29.♕b2

29.♖xf7 is met by 29...♘e5 30.♖f8+ ♔d7 (or simply 30...♗e8) 31.♖xa8 ♘xc4, when Black is winning.

29...♕e3 30.♗xf7 ♗b5 31.♖fd1 ♘f5

He might also have taken care of his a8-rook with the fittingly Steinitzian 31...♔d7.

32.a4 ♘e5

White was poised to meet 32...♗xa4 with 33.♖e2, although even this would leave Black with all the winning chances.

33.axb5 ♘xf7 34.♖e2 ♕h6

Of all the possible retreats, Steinitz prefers the one involving a threat.

35.♕b3

White hasn't exhausted all of his counterplay possibilities, and presses his desperate attack. Black's first job is to consolidate his forces.

35...axb5

There are some interesting variations after 35...♕h5 36.♖de1 ♘e5 37.g4! – again, the best practical chance, although an insufficient one after 37...♕xg4 38.♕g8+ ♔d7 39.♕xa8 ♕f3+ 40.♔g1 axb5.

36.g4!

Sharpening play to the utmost. Black must now play very accurately.

36...♘d4!

It can be very dangerous to be a hostage to extra material. Experienced players can sense exactly when they need to give up their material advantage. Weaker players try to hold onto it at any cost, which often is what causes them to lose. Steinitz sacrifices his knight both to consolidate his forces and to launch a vicious attack on the white king's position.

37.♖xd4 ♖a1+ 38.♔g2 ♕f6 39.♖de4 ♘e5 40.♖f2 ♕g6 41.♖ef4 c6 42.♕e3 ♔c7 43.h3 h5

That's all there is to it. Black can also think about steadily advancing the queenside pawns with 43...c5.

44.♖f5 hxg4 45.♖g5 gxh3+

Strangely, this natural move complicates matters for Black. Instead 45...♕h6 or 45...♕h7 are worth considering.

46.♔h2 ♖a3

Played in the spirit of the Steinitz in those days: not one step back! For the sake of analysis, it's interesting to see what would have happened had the queen retreated: 46...♕e8 47.♖xg7+ ♔b8 48.♕d4. Now White's game, it would seem, just glides along. But Black's resources are not yet exhausted. In fact, chess contains in it some unbelievable possibilities. It would appear as though White has Black wrapped in his coils; all that's needed is a couple of precise moves, and Black's whole position will collapse. But look at this variation: 48...♖a4!! 49.♕xd6+ ♔a7 50.♕c5+ ♔a6 51.♖f8 ♘d3!!:

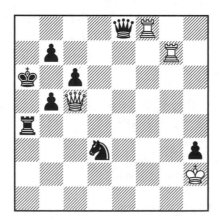

– and suddenly, it is White who has to think about finding a way to save himself – a change which, in a practical game, it is very hard to adjust to.

After the game move we reach an unusual endgame.

47.♕xe5 dxe5 48.♖xg6 b4 49.♖b2

And why not 49.♖xg7+ ♔b6 50.♖ff7, tying Black down at least temporarily to the pawn's defense? Because Black would have replied 50...♖a7.

49...c5 50.♖f2 ♖d3 51.♖c2?

Fritz suggests 51.♖e2 or 51.♖f5 here, with saving chances.

51...b6 52.♖e6

Here, *Fritz* also recommends 52.♖f2 or 52.♖xg7+. After the text move, White is lost.

52...b3 53.♖b2 c4 54.♖xe5 ♔c6 55.♖g5 ♖d5 56.♖xg7 ♔c5 57.♔xh3 ♔b4 58.♖b1 b5 59.♖g4 ♖d2 60.♖g5 b2 61.♔g3 c3 62.♔f3 ♔c4 63.♖gg1 ♔b3 64.♔e3 ♖d8 65.♖gf1 c2 66.♔e2 ♔a2 0-1

A captivating encounter, teaching us how to attack, to sacrifice material, and to counterattack! In the opening, the great Steinitz was able to demonstrate the viability of his early queen sortie to h4. White could put up no serious opposition against 10...♕d4. Maybe he needs to recapture on d2 with the knight? And one more extremely important note: in commenting on this game, under no circumstances did we set out to criticize either of the two players. We sought only to show some variations to help present an overall picture of the battle.

18. C. Golmayo – W. Steinitz

Match (4), La Habana 1883
Scotch Game C45

1.e4 e5 2.♘f3 ♘c6 3.d4 exd4 4.♘xd4 ♛h4 5.♘b5 ♛xe4+ 6.♗e2 ♗b4+ 7.♗d2

7.♘1c3 is also possible.

7...♔d8 8.0-0 ♗xd2

8...a6 is worth a look.

9.♘xd2

This is the move we mentioned in our notes to Game 17. By transposition, the same position (up to 8...♗xd2) was reached as in that game.

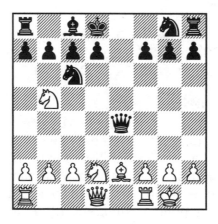

9...♛f4 10.♘b3

This knight could also be used on the kingside. 10.g3 deserves consideration.

10...♘ge7 11.g3 ♕f6 12.c3 h5!

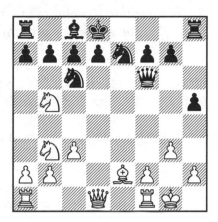

Excellent! In place of the normal 12...d6, Steinitz undertakes active operations on the kingside, targeting the g3-pawn. But this is not the only idea behind the move.

13.♕d2 h4 14.♖ad1 ♕h6!

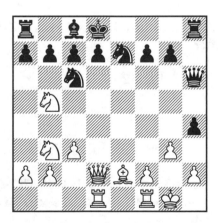

And here it is – the other idea! We already know that trading queens is part of Black's plan.

15.♘c5 ♕xd2 16.♖xd2

Now Black needs to complete development. Note that, with the queens off the board, White is powerless to interfere with this process.

16...b6 17.♘e4 hxg3 18.fxg3 f6 19.♖fd1 a6 20.♘d4 ♘xd4 21.♖xd4 ♘c6 22.♖d5 ♘e5 23.♘g5 ♔e7 24.♘f3 d6

All that remains for Black to do is to cash in on his material advantage.

25.♖5d2 ♗b7 26.♘xe5 fxe5 27.♗c4 ♖af8 28.a4 ♖f6 29.a5 b5 30.♗f1 d5 31.♗g2 c6 32.b3 ♖d8 33.c4 ♖fd6 34.cxb5 cxb5 35.♖c1 e4

35...♖c6 is simpler.

36.♖dc2 d4?

Better is 36...♔f6.

37.♖c7+ ♖8d7 38.♗h3 ♗d5 39.♖xd7+ ♖xd7 40.♗xd7 ♔xd7 41.♖d1 d3 42.♔f2?

The battle continues after 42.b4.

42...♗xb3

Now it's merely a matter of technique.

43.♖d2 ♗c2 44.♔e3 b4 45.♖f2 b3 46.♖f7+ ♔c6 47.♖xg7 b2 48.♖g6+ ♔c5 49.♖b6 b1♕ 50.♖xb1 ♗xb1 51.h4 ♗a2 52.g4 ♗f7 53.h5 ♔c4 0-1

19. C. Golmayo – W. Steinitz

Match (6), La Habana 1883
Scotch Game C45

**1.e4 e5 2.♘f3 ♘c6 3.d4 exd4 4.♘xd4 ♕h4 5.♘b5 ♕xe4+
6.♗e2 ♗b4+ 7.♗d2 ♔d8 8.0-0 ♗xd2 9.♕xd2 a6 10.♘5c3 ♕h4**

Sometimes, in this sort of situation, Steinitz would successfully play the more enterprising and to-the-point 10...♕d4. It is difficult to answer the question as to why, for this game, he preferred a different approach. Quite often, chessplayers will make their choice based on psychological considerations.

11.♘a3

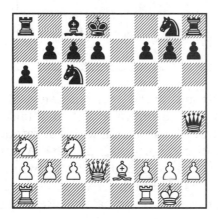

From our perspective, 11.♘d5, freeing c3 for the other knight, is interesting.

11...b5

The first world champion takes the same approach as in Game 16 and the contest takes on a forcing character. And we know how dangerous Steinitz could be in hand-to-hand combat.

12.♗f3

Golmayo accepts the challenge, but his move meets with a powerful rejoinder, as though it were taken directly from the previous game between these two opponents (see Black's move 14 in Game 18). Here too, 12.♘d5 doesn't look too bad.

12...♕h6!

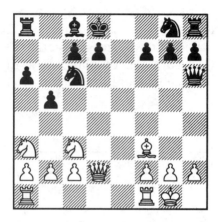

Forceful and strong. In the previous game, Steinitz combined the idea of a favorable queen trade with an attack on the h-pawn; in this game, the trade is associated with a different concept – winning one of the white knights with ...b5-b4. A multitude of ideas in the same move is one sign that it's a strong move. Such a thing is seen in many forms of human activity. And in chess, this sort of thing is most often seen in combinations. Recall the famous study by Richard Réti:

R. Réti

(*Ostrauer Morgenzeitung*, 4 December 1921)

(*see diagram next page*)

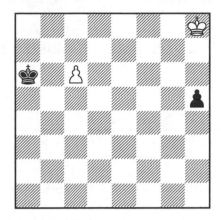

Switching back and forth between two ideas – the threat of entering the square of the black pawn, and aiming to support its own pawn – the white king achieves the draw: 1.♔g7 ♔b6 (1...h4 2.♔f6 h3 3.♔e7 or 3.♔e6, draw) 2.♔f6 h4 3.♔e5 h3 4.♔d6=.

It's interesting that Steinitz's opponent twice overlooked (see the previous game) the same strong queen maneuver. When that happens, we say: he (White) tripped twice over the same rock.

13.♖ad1

Allowing the exchange of queens, which amounts to a little victory for Black in this opening. It seems to us that White might have tried to stir up complications with 13.♕e2. Now 13...b4 would be very dangerous for Black, since he would come under a very strong attack after 14.♖fe1, for instance 14...♘ge7 (14...♕e6 allows the pretty queen maneuver 15.♕d3! ♕g6 16.♕e3! ♕e6 17.♕c5!) 15.♘d5!. However, an entertaining struggle ensues after 13...♗b7.

Now Black obtains a pleasant ending and, exploiting his opponent's missteps, brings the game to victory.

13...♕xd2 14.♖xd2 ♘ge7 15.♘d5 ♖b8 16.♖e1 d6 17.♖de2 ♗e6 18.♘f4? ♘d4 19.♖e4 ♘xf3+ 20.gxf3 ♘f5 21.♘xe6+ fxe6 22.♖xe6 b4!

Dotting the "i". Greater loss of material for White is now unavoidable.

23.♘c4 ♘d4 24.♖6e3 ♘xc2 25.♘a5 ♖b5 26.♘c6+ ♔d7 27.♘a7 ♖g5+ 0-1

20. C. Golmayo – W. Steinitz

Match (1), La Habana 1883
Scotch Game C45

1.e4 e5 2.♘f3 ♘c6 3.d4 exd4 4.♘xd4 ♕h4 5.♘f3

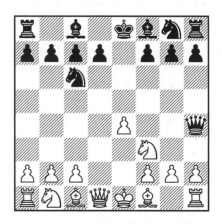

5...♕xe4+

Steinitz takes up the challenge – which is totally logical: the humble 5...♕h5 guarantees White a peaceful, comfortable life. Besides, then why play 4...♕h4 in the first place?

6.♗e2 ♗b4+!? 7.c3 ♗e7 8.0-0 ♘f6 9.♖e1 ♕d5 10.♘d4 ♘xd4

One might also suggest 10...0-0, although that would not alter the overall picture of the game: Black will experience difficulties while White will have clear, easy play. We think that Golmayo would have been able to set difficult problems for Black. The position requires conscientious analysis in order to answer the question: can Black escape unscathed from the complications of this opening?

Let the reader dissect this position: analyzing positions like this can only increase your level of mastery. Did you know that the fifth world champion, Max Euwe of the Netherlands, in his day analyzed a boatload of critical positions, which – in the opinion of specialists – was the reason for his rise through the chess ranks? It was no accident that he was the only one ever to defeat Alexander Alekhine in a title match.

11.cxd4

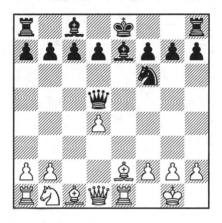

11...0-0

This natural move leads to a difficult position for Black. It is hard to blame Steinitz for not finding the following, far from obvious, defensive plan: 11...♕a5 (with the idea of freeing the d5 square for the pawn) followed by ...♗c8-e6. You'll agree that such a fancy plan isn't all that easy to notice, especially with the clock ticking! I will say this: when *Fritz* suggested 11...♕a5 as best, at first we did not see the defensive point behind it.

Now White gains an advantage big enough to win.

12.♗f3 ♕d6 13.b3! ♗d8 14.♗a3 ♕b6 15.♗c5 ♕a6 16.♗xf8 ♔xf8 17.♘c3 ♕a5 18.♘e4

18.♕d3 is better. Black now gets counterplay.

18...d5 19.♘xf6 ♗xf6 20.♗g4 c5 21.♗xc8 ♖xc8 22.♖c1

22.♕h5 is more active.

22...♗xd4 23.♕g4 ♕d8!

A good defensive move. The fight flares up anew.

24.♖ed1 ♖c6 25.b4!

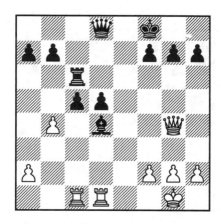

Black must pay attention since, in many variations, he has to consider the capture of the d4-bishop. The position has reached a critical point.

25...♖g6 26.♕f5 ♖f6 27.♕xh7 ♖h6

We can understand Steinitz here: after a difficult defense, he is not averse to a draw or to simplifying into an equal ending. The alternative 27...♗xf2+ 28.♔h1 ♗e3 29.♖c2 leaves the position still at a boil.

28.♕f5 ♖f6 29.♕h7 ♖h6 30.♕c2 ♕h4 31.h3 ♖f6 32.♖xd4

To some extent forced, since 32.♖d2 c4 guarantees Black a very pleasant game.

32...♕xd4 33.♕xc5+ ♕xc5 34.♖xc5

Steinitz has achieved equality! Later on, however, he unexpect-edly takes the game into a pawn ending where his opponent can create an outside passed pawn on the kingside, with excellent winning chances. No doubt Steinitz totally understood the kind of position he was going into, but it seems that he committed an inaccuracy in his calculations. What can you do? Even the greatest players can make mistakes.

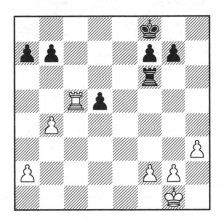

34...♖a6 35.♖a5 ♖xa5 36.bxa5 ♔e7 37.♔f1 ♔d6 38.♔e2 ♔c5 39.♔d3 d4 40.h4 f5 41.g3 ♔d5 42.f3 ♔e5 43.h5 ♔d5 44.a3 a6 45.a4 ♔e5 46.♔c4 d3 47.♔xd3 ♔d5 48.g4 fxg4 49.fxg4 ♔e5 50.♔e3 ♔e6 51.♔e4 ♔f6 52.♔f4 ♔e6 53.g5 ♔e7 54.♔e5 1-0

21. A. Nadanian – N. Short

Playchess.com (3 min. + 1 sec.) 2006
Queen's Pawn Game A40

An unexpected king move decides a game between Ashot Na-danian and Nigel Short.

1.d4 e6 2.e4 ♘f6 3.e5 ♘d5 4.c4 ♗b4+?

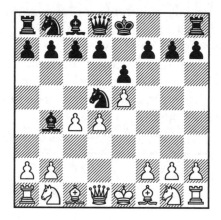

5.♔e2!!

White wins a piece; he won the game on move 25.

22. I. Nepomniachtchi – D. Loskutov

Moscow 2010
Sicilian Defense B90

1.e4 c5 2.♘f3 d6 3.d4 cxd4 4.♘xd4 ♘f6 5.♘c3 a6 6.♗e3 e5 7.♘b3 ♗e7 8.♕d2!

I admit it: there's something nice about the fact that there can be something else besides the English Attack – the more so, when employed by a youngster. In fact, despite his youth, Ian Nepomniachtchi already knows very well how to handle his king (recall his game against Grischuk earlier in this chapter).

8...♘g4 9.g3! ♘xe3 10.♕xe3 ♗g5 11.f4 exf4 12.gxf4 ♗h4+

(see diagram next page)

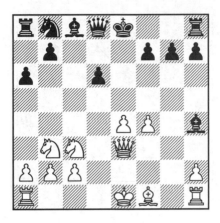

13.♔d2

The temporary discomfort suffered by White's king is fully compensated for by his beautiful pawn center, by his control of the central strong point d5, and by other advantages (in space, for example), plus the weak d6-pawn.

13...0-0 14.♖d1 ♝e6 15.♔c1

Compared to Steinitz's games, White has solved the problem of his king quite quickly. Now play enters an interesting phase, where White begins pressing against the weak d6-pawn with all of his major pieces. Meanwhile, Black pins his hopes on the two bishops and on tactics.

15...♞c6 16.♖g1 ♛e7 17.♛d2 a5 18.♝b5 ♖fd8 19.♔b1 ♝f6 20.♝a4 ♔h8 21.♖g3 g6 22.a3

White passes on the very strong move 22.♞d5!?.

22...♝g7 23.♖d3 ♛h4 24.♝xc6 bxc6

(see diagram next page)

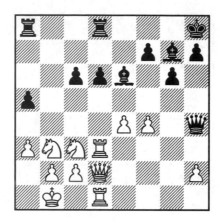

25.e5

We're assuming that taking on d6 might not have appealed to White because of 25...⬛xd6 26.♕xd6 ♝xc3; although even here, White's chances would have been superior. By blocking the center, however, Nepomniachtchi pins his hopes on the capabilities of his knights.

25...a4 26.♘c1

26.♘c5 is more in the spirit of things.

26...♝g4 27.⬛g1 d5 28.⬛d4

Winning a pawn, but it's still not clear how the game will turn out. Black does have his trumps.

28...♝f5 29.♘xa4 ♝f8

Had Black played 29...⬛db8! here, it would still be unclear whether White's pawn outweighed Black's initiative.

30.♘b3 ⬛db8 31.⬛g3! ⬛b5 32.⬛c3!

White carries on the battle forcefully and consistently. Within a couple of moves, he completely paralyzes his opponent's pieces, blockading Black's pair of center pawns. And in such cases, knights outweigh bishops. We recommend to young chessplayers that they study the way White carries out the decisive attack.

32...♕e7 33.♘ac5 ♖ab8 34.♔a2 ♕a7 35.♖a4! ♕b6 36.♖a6 ♕c7 37.♕d4 ♗c8 38.♖a4 ♕b6 39.e6+ ♗g7

Beautifully played. White is winning.

40.exf7 ♗f5 41.♖e3

An unfortunate oversight. 41.♕e3 wins easily, as on 41...♖f8 White has 42.♖a8. Once again, Black's position becomes playable.

41...♖f8 42.♖e5 ♗xc2 43.♕c3 ♗xb3+

43...♖xc5 doesn't look bad here, and Black should have a decent game.

44.♘xb3 d4?!

Evidently, the eighth rank had to be protected with 44...♕b8.

45.♘xd4 ♖xe5 46.fxe5 ♗xe5 47.♕e3 ♗g7?

Ruins the game. After 47...♕c5, White stands better, but the struggle continues. Now comes the dénouement.

48.♖a8 ♕c5 49.♖xf8+ ♗xf8 50.♔b1 ♗e7 51.♕f4 h5 1-0

Illustrative Games

1. The Aggressive King

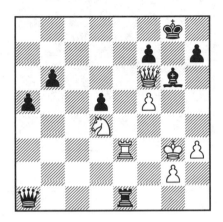

A. Morozevich – L. Aronian

Morelia/Linares 2007

Black's position is quite difficult. With his last move (...♖h1-e1), he defends against mate.

1.♖f3

White wins with 1.♕d8+ ♔g7 2.f6+ ♔h6 3.♔h4! (aggressive king) 3...♕xd4+ 4.g4+.

1...♖f1 2.fxg6

White misses another chance to win, this time with 2.♕d8+ ♔g7 3.f6+ ♔h6 4.♔h4! ♕xd4+ (4...♕e1+ 5.g3 ♕e4+ 6.g4 ♕e1+ 7.♖g3) 5.g4 threatening ♕f8#, and if 5...♕c5, then 6.♕f8+! ♕xf8 7.g5#. Now Black can save himself.

2...♖xf3+ 3.♕xf3 ♕e1+ 4.♔f4 hxg6 5.♕xd5 ♕f2+ 6.♘f3 ♕xg2 ½-½

2. Evacuating the King Before the Opponent's Attack Breaks Through

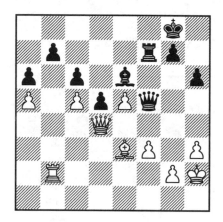

M. Carlsen – S. Karjakin

World Chp (5), New York 2016

White can count on winning if he advances the kingside pawns. Therefore, Black runs his king to the opposite flank.

32...♚f8 33.♕c3 ♚e8 34.♖b4 g5

It's easier to play this kind of move when your king is far away.

35.♖b2 ♚d8 36.♖f2 ♚c8 37.♕d4 ♕g6

Black rightly doesn't sit around waiting, but instead prepares a pawn break. This explains the world champion's reply.

38.g4 h5 39.♕d2 ♖g7 40.♚g3 ♖g8 41.♚g2 hxg4 42.hxg4 d4

Played in classical style, although after 42...♕h6 it would have been possible to disturb the opponent's king. Black naturally wishes to include the bishop in the attack.

43.♕xd4 ♗d5 44.e6

Like 42...d4, another anti-blockading move. Black's example has become infectious.

White doesn't want to wait and simply defend, for example 44.♔g3 ♕b1 45.♕d2 ♕g1, and it looks like both sides must acquiesce to the draw: 46.♖g2 ♕f1.

44...♕xe6 45.♔g3 ♕e7 46.♖h2 ♕f7

Black decides not to play 46...♕c7+ to capture the a5-pawn. Here we have to assume that if the black king had run all the way to a8, then maybe Karjakin would have chosen this line. Now, however, we get simplifications and the draw becomes inevitable.

47.f4 gxf4+ 48.♕xf4 ♕e7 49.♖h5 ♖f8 50.♖h7 ♖xf4 51.♖xe7 ♖e4 ½-½

Curiously, *Rybka* evaluates the final position as +0.69, while it's plain to see that Black draws easily.

3. The Active King

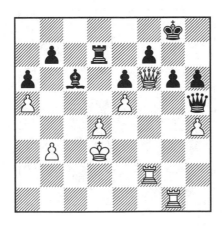

J. Gallagher – E. Aranovitch

Bürgenstock (Switzerland) Open 2003

Earlier in the battle, White managed to "stalemate" part of his opponent's forces. Only the bishop and the king can move (honestly, without anything particular to do), and Black is reduced to treading water. So how should White proceed? His pieces occupy excellent squares and it's almost impossible to improve them. Improbably, the game is decided by the king's wonderful dash! It penetrates the opponent's camp, latches onto the rook, and then comes the long-awaited break!

1.♔c4! ♔h7 2.♔c5 ♔g8

2...♗e4 3.♔b6 ♔g8 4.♔a7 g5 5.hxg5 ♕g6 6.♕xg6+ fxg6 7.♖f4 ♗d3 8.gxh6 doesn't save Black either.

3.♔b6 ♔h7 4.♔a7 ♔g8 5.♔b8 ♔h7 6.♔c8 ♔g8 7.d5 exd5 8.e6 fxe6 9.♖xg6+ ♔h7 10.♖fg2 1-0

4. The King Defends Vulnerable Squares and Runs Away at the Same Time

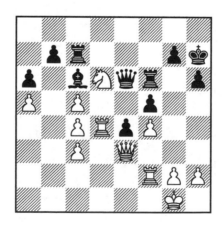

S. Tiviakov – A. Moiseenko

Montréal 2009

White is clearly better, but he cannot make progress without a pawn break on the kingside. In this case, it's better to move the king to the other flank. GM Tiviakov finds the wonderful b4 square for the king, from where it will defend its pawns, which are in need of support. Very thematic: coordinating the king's evacuation before we launch our pawn storm and using the king to defend vulnerable pawns.

28.♔f1 ♕e7 29.♔e1 ♖d7 30.♖b2 ♖f8 31.♔d1 ♖c7 32.♔c1 ♕h4 33.g3 ♕h3 34.♖f2 ♖e7 35.♔b2 ♔h8 36.♔a3 ♔h7 37.♔b4

The first part of the plan is accomplished; the vulnerable pawns are now held. Now White finds the best redeployment of his pieces and proceeds with the second part of the plan.

37...♔h8 38.♖d1 ♔h7 39.♖e1 ♔h8 40.♕d4 ♔h7 41.♖e3 ♕h5 42.♕d2 ♖d7 43.♕e1 ♕h3 44.♕g1

44.♕e2 is worth a look.

44...♕h5 45.♖g2 ♖f6 46.h3 ♕g6 47.♖d2

If 47.g4, then 47...♖fxd6 48.gxf5 ♕xg2 49.♕xg2 ♖f6 with unclear play, although *Rybka* evaluates White's chances very highly. We think that Black can hold. The strong passer on e4 supported by the bishop, in addition to the weak white pawns and the decent degree of coordination between Black's rooks, can make up for the material imbalance. But this is just our personal opinion. This position requires thorough analysis.

47...♖f8 48.♕d1 ♕e6 49.♖d4 ♖e7 50.♕h5 ♕f6 51.♖d2 ♖e6 52.♕d1 ♖d8 53.g4

Here comes the break!

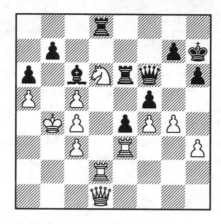

53...fxg4 54.f5

54.♕xg4 looks interesting.

54...♖e5 55.hxg4 ♕e7 56.♖d4 ♕c7?

This loses impressively. *Rybka* suggests 56...♖b8, when White will still need to work hard to achieve the win. Tiviakov thinks that on move 56 White should have played ♖a2, giving long variations in *Chess Assistant*.

57.♘f7!! ♖de8

The main idea is revealed after 57...♖xc5 58.♖xd8 ♕xa5+ 59.♔b3, when Black cannot win the white queen due to the mate on h8. White's advantage could have been converted in other ways. Tiviakov chooses the one that limits Black's counterplay to zero.

58.♘xe5 ♖xe5 59.♖d5 ♗xd5 60.cxd5 ♖e8 61.d6 ♕f7 62.♕b3 ♕d7 63.♕a4 ♕f7 64.♔a3 ♖c8 65.♕d4 ♕d7 66.♖xe4 ♕b5 67.♖e7 ♕xa5+ 68.♔b2 ♕b5+ 69.♔c1 ♖g8 70.d7 ♕f1+ 71.♔d2 ♕g2+ 72.♖e2 1-0

5. The King's Evacuation Facilitates Major-Piece Coordination

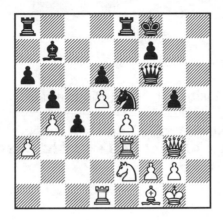

V. Malakhatko – A. Volokitin

Ukrainian Chp, Kharkov 2004

Black transfers the king to the other side, ensuring good coordination between the major pieces. The move can also be explained by the fact that White has the constant threat of f2-f4 and Black's monarch has nothing to do on that side of the board except get into trouble.

30...♔e7

Rybka rates 30...♗c8 more highly than the game move but, as we have mentioned, White can continue 31.f4 gxf4 32.♘xf4, which does not enter into Black's plans. Here we clearly see the difference between a human's and a chess engine's approaches. Black doesn't want to abandon his initial plan, which is understandable in human terms. The engine's line requires much exertion and anxiety, as well as deep, accurate calculation.

31.♘d4 ♖h8 32.♘f5+ ♔d7 33.♖c3 ♔c7 34.♕e3 ♗c8

The king defends White's entry squares, the bishop evicts the f5-knight from its wonderful post, and the game proceeds to its final phase.

35.f3

If 35.♘d4, then 35...♗d7.

Now Black transitions to a victorious attack.

35...♗xf5 36.exf5 ♕xf5 37.♖d4 ♕b1 38.♕xg5 ♖ag8 39.♕e7+ ♔c8 40.♖d2 ♖h1+ 41.♔xh1 ♕xf1+ 42.♔h2 ♖h8+ 43.♔g3 ♕e1+ 44.♖f2 ♖g8+ 0-1

6. The King Finds Safe Haven (I)

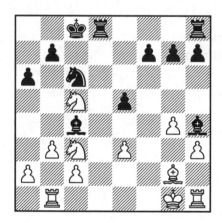

D. Navara – R. Wojtaszek

Biel 2015

19...♗g5 20.♔f2 ♗h4+ 21.♔f3

After 21.♔g1 we would have a repetition. Now White sends his king into Black's camp. A risky idea. The king, traveling along a treacherous path in the midst of Black's army, goes all the way to the eighth rank!

21...e4+!?

Black accepts the challenge; now we will see some entertaining play. After 21...♗d5+ 22.♘xd5 ♖xd5 23.♘e4, the game is equal.

22.♔f4!?

22.♘3xe4 ♘e5+ 23.♔f4 ♘g6+ 24.♔f3 ♘e5+ leads to a draw. However, the GMs decide to play on some more.

22...g5+ 23.♔f5 ♖he8 24.♖hd1 ♖e5+ 25.♔f6 ♖g8!?

Black decides to attack the reckless king. Quiet play ensues after 25...♖xc5, or 25...♖xd1 26.♖xd1 ♖xc5 27.♘a4 with equal chances.

26.bxc4 ♖g6+ 27.♔xf7 ♖e7+ 28.♔f8 ♖f6+ 29.♔g8 ♖g6+ 30.♔h8!?

The placement of White's king begs for a diagram:

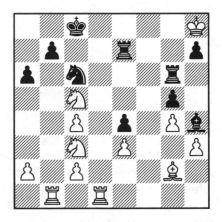

30...♖f6 31.♖f1 ♗f2 32.♖xf2

The following sharp variation leads to a draw: 32.♘e6 ♖exe6 33.♗xe4 (33.♘xe4 ♖f7) 33...♖e7 34.♗f5+ ♔b8 35.♔g8 ♖ef7. White decides to dial back the tension and the game enters still waters with mutual chances (although slightly better for White). Even so, we clearly see the superiority of White's king over Black's.

32...♖xf2 33.♖f1 ♖xg2?

It was imperative to defend the back rank before making this capture: 33...♖e8+ 34.♔xh7 ♖xg2, when after 35.♘3xe4 we get a complicated endgame, where it's difficult to evaluate the position and figure out which side has the better prospects.

34.♖f8+ ♔c7 35.♘d5+

Stronger is 35.♘5xe4!, with threats. Please note the wonderful coordination between the rook and the two knights. After the game move, Black finds counterplay and we get a race to see who will promote first.

35...♔d6 36.♘xe7 ♔xc5 37.♖f5+ ♔xc4 38.♘xc6 bxc6 39.♖xg5 ♖g3 40.h4 h6 41.♖g6 ♖xe3 42.♔g7 ♖g3 43.♔xh6 e3 44.♔g5 ♔d5

The alternative also leads to a difficult position: 44...♔c3 45.♖e6 (45.♖xc6+ ♔d2 46.♖d6+ ♔xc2 47.h5 e2 48.♖e6 ♔d2 49.h6).

45.♔f4

45.♖g8!.

45...♖h3?

The stubborn 45...e2 offers better chances for salvation, for example 46.c4+ ♔xc4 47.♖xc6+ (47.♖e6 ♖h3 48.♖xe2 ♖xh4) 47...♔d5 48.♖c1. Now the game comes to an end.

46.h5 c5 47.♖g5+ ♔d4 48.♖e5 1-0

Next, we see a fearless king moving to the middle of the board because other lines failed to meet the requirements of the situation. But to call this a "safe harbor" would be (to put it mildly) an exaggeration. This example is very striking and shows that it is not so easy to exploit this king's position.

7. The King Finds Safe Haven (II)

A. Karpov – A. Zaitsev

Russian Chp, Kuibyshev 1970

1.e4 c6 2.d4 d5 3.♘c3 dxe4 4.♘xe4 ♘d7 5.♘f3 ♘gf6 6. ♘xf6+ ♘xf6 7.♘e5 ♗f5 8.c3 e6 9.g4 ♗g6 10.h4 ♗d6 11.♕e2 c5 12.h5 ♗e4 13.f3 cxd4 14.♕b5+ ♘d7

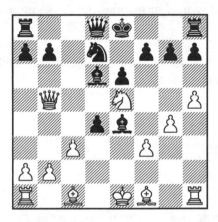

Anatoly Karpov showed great form in this tournament and deservedly won the title of Champion of Russia. In this particular game, he plays the opening very aggressively against Alexander Zaitsev. GM Zaitsev (who died too young) brilliantly rebuffs White's threats; in the diagram position he induces Karpov into making the following move, after which the white king is forced to march all the way up to e4!

15.♘xf7 ♗g3+ 16.♔e2 d3+

In his book *My Best Games*, Karpov says he intended to reply to 16...♕f6 with 17.fxe4 ♕xf7 18.♕d3 ♕f2+ 19.♔d1 0-0, with a very bad position.

17.♔e3

A brave decision. The safer 17.♔d2 leads to a difficult position after 17...♔xf7 18.fxe4 ♘e5 19.♔d1 ♖f8.

Also possible is 19...d2 20.♗xd2 ♗f4 21.♕e2 ♘c4.

17...♕f6

About this move, Karpov writes that Zaitsev was trying to squeeze the most out of the position. After the stronger 17...♔xf7, however, White faces insurmountable problems. White intended to answer this move with 18.♔xe4 ♘f6+ (18...a6 19.♕xb7 ♕e7 is a strong reply here) 19.♔e3 ♘d5+ 20.♔e4, although *Rybka* figures that Black should win after either Karpov's suggestion 20...♖c8 or the stronger 20...♕d6.

The evaluation is the same after 20.♔d2 ♗f4+ 21.♔d1 d2. Now we see the king march forward!

18.♔xe4

The only move! 18.fxe4 ♕xf7 19.♔xd3 ♕f3+ is completely pathetic.

18...♕xf7 19.♖h3

The other way to defend the h3-pawn, 19.♗g2, leads to a more difficult position after 19...a6.

19...a6 20.♕g5 h6

Looks threatening. Apparently Black was only counting on 21.♕g6 ♘c5+ 22.♔e3 (22.♔d4 0-0-0+) 22...♗f4+ 23.♔f2 ♕xg6 24.hxg6 d2, with an easy win.

Meanwhile, with 20...e5 21.♖xg3 ♘c5+ 22.♔e3 0-0 23.♗xd3 (23. ♖h3 ♖ad8) 23...♕f4+ 24.♕xf4 exf4+ 25.♔d4 ♘xd3 26.♖g1 ♖ad8+ 27.♔c4 ♘e5+, Black can keep fighting for the win, even though White still retains drawing chances.

21.♕e3!

The future world champion shows his class!

A picturesque position – the king is at the head of his army!

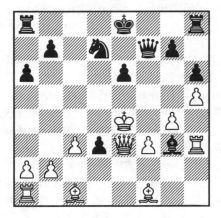

The obvious 21...♘f6+ 22.♔xd3 ♘xg4 23.fxg4 ♕xf1+ 24.♔c2 ♕xh3 leads to perpetual check after 25.♕xe6+. It's hard to believe it, but White has equalized.

21...e5 22.♔xd3 ♗f4 23.♕g1

The point of this move is to keep the knight off c5, although the simple 23.♕e1 is not bad either.

23...0-0-0 24.♔c2 ♗xc1 25.♖xc1! ♕xa2 26.♖h2

Better is 26.♗d3.

26...♖hf8

26...e4 is interesting.

27.♖d2 ♕a4+

On 27...♖xf3, Karpov intended to place the bishop on the long diagonal and to double the rooks on the d-file.

28.♔b1 ♕c6 29.♗d3 ♔c7?

This is now a mistake. It was imperative to play 29...♘c5 30.♗f5+ ♔b8 with an almost equal game, White's chances being a shade better. From now on, White increases his initiative and – exploiting his opponent's inaccuracies – confidently guides the game to victory.

30.♗e4± ♕b6 31.♔h2 ♖de8 32.♖cd1 ♘f6 33.♗g6 ♖e7 34.♖e1 ♕b5 35.♖de2 ♘d7 36.♗f5 ♖xf5 37.gxf5 ♕d3+ 38.♔a1 ♕xf5 39.♕h4 ♘f6 40.♕c4+ ♔d8 41.♕c5 ♘d7 42.♕d5 ♔c8 43.♖e4 b5 44.♕a8+ ♔c7 45.♕a7+ ♔d8 46.♕xa6 ♕xh5 47.f4 ♕f5 48.♕a8+ ♔c7 49.♕a5+ ♔c6 50.c4 b4 51.♕xb4 ♖e6 52.fxe5 ♔c7 53.♕a5+ ♔b7 54.♕b5+ ♖b6 55.♕d5+ ♔c7 56.♔b1 ♕f2 57.♖4e2 ♕f5+ 58.♕e4 ♕xe4+ 59.♖xe4 ♘c5 60. ♖4e3 ♘e6 61.♔c2 g5 62.♔c3 h5 63.b4 ♖a6 64.c5 ♖a3+ 65.♔c4 ♖xe3 66.♖xe3 h4 67.b5 ♔d8 68.b6 ♔d7 69.♖d3+ ♔c8 70.♖d6 h3 71.♖xe6 g4 72.♖h6 1-0

8. The Active King

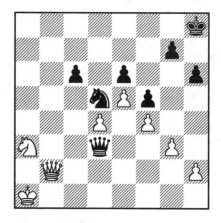

E. Akhmilovskaya – N. Alexandria

Candidates' Match (Women) (6), Kislovodsk 1980

I remember Mark Dvoretsky showing this position after the match, in which he served as Alexandria's second. In this adjourned position, he analyzed many continuations but found counterplay for White everywhere he looked. Then all of a sudden, an idea appeared: could we attack the h2-pawn with our king? If the answer is in the affirmative, then White's entire kingside pawn chain will disintegrate. Analysis showed that White will lack serious counterplay and that this is the surest path to victory. The game ended within a few moves.

41...♔h7 42.♘b1 ♔g6 43.♕d2 ♕xd2 44.♘xd2 ♔h5 45. ♘c4

No better is 45.h3 g5 46.fxg5 hxg5 47.♔b1 g4.

45...♔g4 46.♘a5 ♘e7 47.♔b2 ♔h3 48.♔c3 ♔xh2 49.♔c4 ♔xg3 50.♔c5 h5 51.♔d6 ♘d5 52.♔xe6 h4 53.♘xc6 ♘xf4+ 54.♔xf5 h3 0-1

Exercises

1. B. Spassky – E. Geller
1959

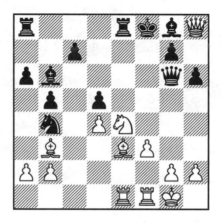

Black to move

2. B. Spassky – E. Geller
1959

White to move

3. V. Anand – J. Timman

1996

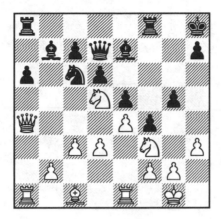

White to move

4. A. Palekha – V. Komliakov

2004

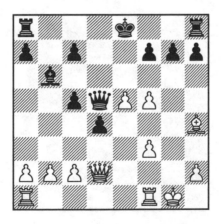

Black to move

5. V. Gavrikov – N. Rashkovsky
1986

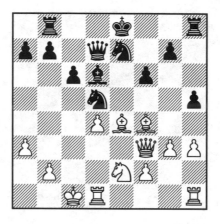

Black to move

6. S. Loyd
1903

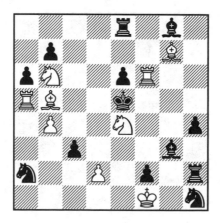

White to move

7. V. Gavrikov – V. Muratov
1977

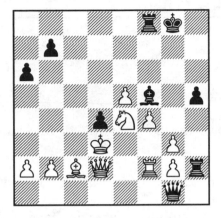

White to move

8. V. Gavrikov – S. Lputian
1980

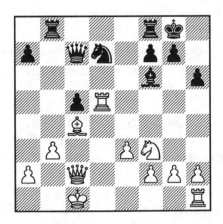

White to move

Solutions

1. B. Spassky – E. Geller

USSR Chp, Tbilisi 1959

In this complex position, Black played:

29...♔f7 30.♗d2 ♗h7

30...♗xd4+ is worth a look: 31.♔h1 ♘d3 32.♗xd5+ ♔e7! 33.♗xa8 ♗e6.

31.♗xb4 ♖xh8 32.♗xd5+ ♔e8 33.♘c5+ ♔d8 34.♗xa8,

and White had compensation. Later on, he even managed to win (see Exercise 2).

If Black had selected the brave 29...♔e7! (the king takes care of its own problems!), Black would probably have won.

2. B. Spassky – E. Geller

USSR Chp, Tbilisi 1959

In this position, Boris Spassky decides to go after Black's passed pawn with his king. Faced with the loss of this vital pawn, Geller gave up after:

65.♗c1 ♕d1 66.♔f4 b4 67.♔e5 b3 68.♔d4 ♕c2 69.♗b2 ♔h8 70.♗c3 ♕a2 71.♗b2 ♕b1 72.♔c3 ♕c2+ 73.♔b4 ♔g8 74.♔a3 ♕c4 75.♘c1 1-0

2a. The above game reminds us of Tal–Portisch, Candidates' Match (2) 1965, where Tal bravely sacrificed a rook for the attack. In reply, Portisch sacrificed the queen back in order to fend off White's dangerous threats.

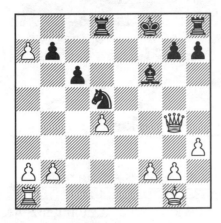

Here GM Portisch, like Spassky in the previous example, decides to attack and remove the dangerous pawn... with his king. But this time, the plan proved insufficient in view of White's numerous threats.

22...♔e7 23.b4 ♖a8 24.♖e1+ ♔d6 25.b5 ♖xa7 26.♖e6+ ♔c7 27.♖xf6 1-0

Although Black lost, the plan itself seems quite original to us, and worthy of study.

3. V. Anand – J. Timman

Amsterdam 1996

Under Black's pawn storm, White evacuates the king from the danger zone. Anand's handling of the king is impressive.

19.♔f1

Another possibility is 19.♘xe7 ♕xe7 20.d4, with the better chances.

19...h5 20.♔e2 g4 21.hxg4 hxg4 22.♘d2 ♔g7 23.♘c4 a5 24.♔d1 ♗h4 25.♖f1 ♖f7 26.♗d2 ♕e6 27.♔c2 ♘d8 28.g3 ♗g5 29.gxf4 exf4 30.♖g1 ♗c6 31.♕a2 ♘b7 32.b4 ♗b5 33.♘xa5

♖xa5 34.bxa5 ♗xd3+ 35.♔xd3 ♘c5+ 36.♔c2 ♕xe4+ 37.♔b2
♘d3+ 38.♔a3 ♘e5 39.♘b4 c5 40.♖ae1 cxb4+ 41.cxb4 ♕d3+
42.♔a4 ♖a7 43.♕b2 ♗f6 44.♗xf4 ♘c4 45.♖xg4+ ♔f7 46.♕b3
♕d5 47.♗d2 1-0

4. A. Palekha – V. Komliakov

Serpukhov 2004

It's not hard to see that Black's main problem is the condition of
his king. Grandmaster Viktor Komliakov resolves that problem in
two moves, getting his king out of the danger zone. The king solves
its own problems.

19...♔d7 20.♗g3 ♔c6 21.♔h1 f6 22.a4 a5 23.exf6 gxf6
24.♕f4 ♖he8 25.♖fe1 c4 26.♖e4 ♖e5 27.♖xe5 fxe5 28.♕e4
♕xe4 29.fxe4 ♗c5 30.♗xe5 ♖e8 31.♗g7 ♖xe4 32.♖f1 d3

Black could have kept playing for the win with 32...♖e2 33.f6
♖xc2 34.f7 d3. Now, though, a draw is the most likely result.

33.cxd3 cxd3 34.♗c3 ♗b4 35.♗xb4 axb4 36.f6 d2 37.f7
♖e1 38.f8♕ d1♕ 39.♕a8+ ♔d7 40.♖xe1 ♕xe1+ 41.♔g2 ♕e2+
42.♔g3 ♕xb2 43.♕d5+ ♔e7 44.♕c5+ ♔e6 45.♕c6+ ♔f5
46.♕d7+ ♔g6 47.♕e6+ ♔g7 48.♕e7+ ½-½

5. V. Gavrikov – N. Rashkovsky

USSR Chp, Kiev 1986

In this example, Black also resolves his king's problems by finding it safe haven.

18...♔d8 19.♗d2 ♖c8 20.♘f4 ♗xf4 21.♗xf4 ♘xf4 22.gxf4
♘d5 23.♖hg1 ♖c7 24.♔b1 ♕d6 25.f5 ♖e7 1-0

6. S. Loyd

1903

A brilliant three-move problem by the legendary American composer Sam Loyd, dedicated to the genius Steinitz. It seems that Loyd was heavily influenced by the first world champion's idea in the Vienna Game. The idea in this problem is truly staggering!

1.♔e2!!

Fantastic! The king decides to take part in the mating attack, not fearing either the double check or the queen promotion!

1...f1♕+ 2.♔e3!!

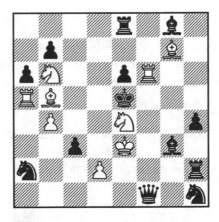

Tightening the noose around his opponent. This is how you can make use of the power of the king!

Now it becomes clear: on every check – and there are ten (!!) of them – White replies with mate.

Anyone who genuinely values the art of chess is bound to feel moved by this treasure. Truly, the human mind is a wonderful thing!

7. V. Gavrikov – V. Muratov

Beltsy 1977

Moldavian GM Viktor Gavrikov senses beautifully how to work with his king in complex positions. Watch this interesting game.

42.♔c4! ♖c8+ 43.♔d5 d3!? 44.♗xd3 ♖d8+ 45.♘d6 ♗xd3 46.f5!! ♔h7 47.f6

47.♔e6!? is also worth considering.

47...♗g6 48.f7

And here too, the king move is strongest: 48.♔e6!?.

48...♕b1?!

Here Black has a hard-to-spot defense: 48...♖xg2! 49.f8♕ (49. ♖xg2 ♗xf7+ 50.♔e4 ♕c5) 49...♖xf8 50.♖xg2 ♕b6 and, in every variation, Black manages to collect a handful of his scattered pieces, with decent chances.

49.♔e6 ♖h1 50.♔e7 ♖h8 51.e6 ♖c1 52.f8♕ ♖c7+ 53.♔d8

The voyage has reached its successful end!

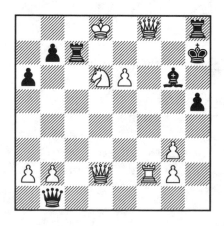

53...♖xf8+ 54.♖xf8 ♖c6 55.♕d4 ♖xd6+ 56.♕xd6 ♕xb2 57.c7 ♕a3 58.♕xa3 1-0

8. V. Gavrikov – S. Lputian

Riga 1980

17.♔d1

White sensibly evacuates his king to the other side. The further course of the game shows that this was enough for equality. However, 17.♔b1!? would have led to a sharp fight, where White's centralized pieces would coordinate better than Black's.

Also, all the major contours of the position favor White. It seems that Gavrikov acted out of general considerations; this is understandable, as it's not easy to make the decision to move the king to the same side where the black bishop, which has no opponent on the dark squares, shows such power.

17...♖fc8 18.♔e2 ♘b6 19.♖d2 ♘xc4 20.♕xc4 ♖b4 21.♕a6 c4 22.bxc4 ♗c3 23.♖c2 ♖b6 24.♕a4 ♖b4 25.♕a6 ♖b6 26.♕a4 ♖b4 ½-½

Afterword

Thus we conclude our interesting journey, in which the most important and contradictory piece plays the lead role. We hope that this book has broadened your perspectives on how to use the king in complex middlegame and opening positions, to the point where you will not be afraid to put your king to use. In addition, we hope that the reader will derive pleasure from our many examples.

Some final notes and conclusions are in order. First, for trainers we recommend not analyzing all the exercises to the very end – sometimes it's better to limit yourself to evaluating the position once the situation has clarified, and then move on to the next exercise. Why is that? I'll try to explain. This way, you'll be focusing on the main purpose of the book – the classification. This is what will have the greatest value from an educational standpoint. Once you have finished examining all eight facets of king play, then you can go back and spend more time on the exercises. Note that we are not trying to force our opinion on you – this is merely a recommendation.

We want to reiterate that the most important aspect of this book is the classification system.

Finally, I'd like to add that, as your author, I derived immense satisfaction from analyzing the games of the first world champion, Wilhelm Steinitz. I hope that your experience will be the same. Equally astounding was the king play of the ninth world champion, Tigran Petrosian, and the twelfth world champion, Anatoly Karpov!